Object Lifecycles

Selected titles from the YOURDON PRESS COMPUTING SERIES
Ed Yourdon, *Advisor*

AUGUST   Joint Application Design
BAUDIN   Manufacturing Systems Analysis with Application to Production Scheduling
BELLIN AND SUCHMAN   Structured Systems Development Manual
BLOCK   The Politics of Projects
BODDIE   Crunch Mode: Building Effective Systems on a Tight Schedule
BOULDIN   Agents of Change: Managing the Introduction of Automated Tools
BRILL   Building Controls into Structured Systems
BRILL   Techniques of EDP Project Management: A Book of Readings
CHANG   Principles of Visual Programming Systems
COAD AND YOURDON   Object-Oriented Analysis, 2/E
COAD AND YOURDON   Object-Oriented Design
CONNELL AND SHAFER   Structured Rapid Prototyping
CONSTANTINE AND YOURDON   Structured Design
DeGRACE AND STAHL   Wicked Problems, Righteous Solutions
DeMARCO   Concise Notes on Software Engineering
DeMARCO   Controlling Software Projects
DeMARCO   Structured Analysis and System Specification
DeSALVO AND LIEBOWITZ   Managing Artificial Intelligence and Expert Systems
FLAVIN   Fundamental Concepts in Information Modeling
FOLLMAN   Business Applications with Microcomputers
FOURNIER   Practical Guide to Structured System Development and Maintenance
FRANTZEN AND McEVOY   A Game Plan for Systems Development
FRENCH   Business Knowledge Investment
GLASS   Software Conflict
GROCHOW   SAA: A Guide to Implementing IBM's Systems Application Architecture
KELLER   The Practice of Structured Analysis: Exploding Myths
KING   Current Practices in Software Development: A Guide to Successful Systems
KING   Project Management Made Simple
LARSON   Interactive Software
LIEBOWITZ AND DeSALVO   Structuring Expert Systems: Domain, Design, and Development
MARTIN   Transaction Processing Facility: A Guide for Application Programmers
McMENAMIN AND PALMER   Essential System Analysis
PAGE-JONES   Practical Guide to Structured Systems Design, 2/E
PINSON   Designing Screen Interfaces in C
PUTNAM AND MYERS   Measures for Excellence: Reliable Software on Time, within Budget
RIPPS   An Implementation Guide to Real-Time Programming
RODGERS   ORACLE®: A Database Developer's Guide
RODGERS   UNIX® Database Management Systems
RUHL   The Programmer's Survival Guide
SHLAER AND MELLOR   Object Lifecycles: Modeling the World in States
SHLAER AND MELLOR   Object-Oriented Systems Analysis: Modeling the World in Data
SHILLER   Software Excellence
TOIGO   Disaster Recovery Planning: Managing Risk and Catastrophe in Information Systems
VESELY   Strategic Data Management: The Key to Corporate Competitiveness
WARD   Systems Development Without Pain
WARD AND MELLOR   Structured Development for Real-Time Systems
YOURDON   Managing the Structured Techniques, 4/E
YOURDON   Managing the System Life Cycle, 2/E
YOURDON   Modern Structured Analysis
YOURDON   Structured Walkthroughs, 4/E
YOURDON   Techniques of Program Structure and Design

Object Lifecycles
Modeling the World in States

Sally Shlaer
Stephen J. Mellor
Project Technology, Inc.

YOURDON PRESS
P T R Prentice Hall
Englewood Cliffs, New Jersey 07632

Library of Congress Cataloging-in-Publication Data

Shlaer, Sally.
    Object lifecycles : modeling the world in states / Sally Shlaer,
  Stephen J. Mellor.
        p.   cm. -- (Yourdon Press computing series)
    Includes bibliographical references and index.
    ISBN 0-13-629940-7
    1. Object-oriented programming. 2. System analysis.   I. Title.
  II. Title: Object life cycles. III. Series.
  QA76.64.S474 1992
  005.1--dc20   91-13591
                                                          CIP

Editorial/production supervision: *Harriet Tellem*
Cover design: *Wanda Lubelska*
Prepress buyer: *Kelly Behr/Mary Elizabeth McCartney*
Manufacturing buyer: *Susan Brunke*
Acquisitions editor: *Paul W. Becker*
Editorial assistant: *Noreen Regina*

 © 1992 by P T R Prentice Hall
Prentice-Hall, Inc.
A Paramount Communications Company
Englewood Cliffs, New Jersey 07632

The publisher offers discounts on this book when ordered
in bulk quantities. For more information, write:
      Special Sales/Professional Marketing
      Prentice-Hall, Inc.
      Professional & Technical Reference Division
      Englewood Cliffs, New Jersey 07632

UNIX is a registered trademark of UNIX System Laboratories, Inc.
in the USA and other countries.

Printed in the United States of America

10   9   8

ISBN 0-13-629940-7

Prentice-Hall International (UK) Limited, *London*
Prentice-Hall of Australia Pty. Limited, *Sydney*
Prentice-Hall Canada Inc., *Toronto*
Prentice-Hall Hispanoamericana, S.A., *Mexico*
Prentice-Hall of India Private Limited, *New Delhi*
Prentice-Hall of Japan, Inc., *Tokyo*
Simon & Schuster Asia Pte. Ltd., *Singapore*
Editora Prentice-Hall do Brasil, Ltda., *Rio de Janeiro*

Contents

3 Lifecycles of Objects

4 Dynamics of Relationships

5 System Dynamics

6 Process Models

7 Domains

8 Managing a Large Domain

Transforming Object-Oriented Analysis into Object-Oriented Design

Appendices

A OODLE: A Language-Independent Notation for Object-Oriented Design

B Using Object-Oriented Analysis with DOD-STD-2167A

Preface

This book presents Object-Oriented Analysis (OOA), a method for identifying the significant entities in a real-world problem and for understanding and explaining how they interact with one another. The method, which is most commonly used in the context of software or systems engineering, is best described in three steps:

Information models. In this step, the focus is on abstracting the conceptual entities in the problem in terms of objects and attributes. The associations that pertain between the entities are formalized in relationships that are based on the policies, rules, and physical laws that prevail in the real world. This step is treated in *Object-Oriented Systems Analysis: Modeling the World in Data* (Prentice Hall, 1988), and is only briefly reviewed in this, the companion book.

State models. The second step of the method is concerned with the behavior of objects and relationships over time. In OOA, each object and relationship has a lifecycle — an orderly pattern of dynamic behavior. We use state models to formalize the lifecycles of both objects and relationships. The state models, which are expressed in state transition diagrams and tables, communicate with one another by means of events, and are organized in layers to make the system of communication orderly and understandable.

Process models. All of the processing required by the problem is contained in the actions of the state models. In this, the third step of the method, the actions are dissected into fundamental and reusable processes, and are depicted by an enhanced form of the traditional data flow diagram — the Action DFD. The processes that are so derived can then be converted directly into operations (methods) of object-oriented design.

Although OOA was originally defined as a method for the analysis of real-time problems (and hence the emphasis on concurrency, synchronous vs. asynchronous communication, and timers), today we find it as useful for MIS applications as for real-time problems. We have seen the method applied successfully to a broad range of problems including banking operations, manufacturing (aircraft engines, circuit boards, semiconductors, and similar products), battlefield simulations, remotely-controlled vehicles, telecommunications systems, credit card billing, advanced computer peripherals, product quality databases, and intelligent laboratory and medical instruments.

While OOA can be presented in a very formal manner, complete with definitions, theorems and lemmas, we have purposefully chosen to direct this presentation to the practicing (and busy) software professional, and have therefore couched the presentation in terms of examples, guidelines, and discussions that can be assimilated fairly quickly. To support the practical, everyday use of the method, we have described OOA work products in some detail: Experience indicates that it is much easier to bring a method into effective practice when software engineers have a clear view of exactly what they are working to produce. Finally, we have supplied a simple organizational framework for project planning, scheduling, on-going assessment of progress, and similar day-to-day technical management tasks.

History of OOA

OOA, as described in this book, started in 1979 with the analysis phase of a large real-time project at Lawrence Berkeley Laboratory. In this project we made extensive use of information models to organize both static and dynamic data. We used state models to investigate isolated problems, but these models were not seen as a standard part of the project's methodology. DeMarco-style data flow diagrams were also employed, and all data appearing on them was correlated with the information model.

From 1980 to 1984, we used information modeling on several large-scale industrial real-time projects. State models were used extensively, but a systematic association between state models and objects had not yet been made. By 1985, we were using state models to model lifecycles of the information model objects. The data flow diagrams had now become more closely connected with the state models, and incorporated data stores that exactly mirrored the information model objects. In 1986-87, we partitioned the data flow diagrams to correspond to lifecycle states, and added the object communication model. The method was then codified in Project Technology's OOA training courses and given its name, as the analysis analogue of the design and programming technology then developing in the object-oriented community.

What's New

Development of the analysis method since 1987 has been concentrated in two areas: (1) improved guidelines for partitioning actions to ensure that the processes so obtained have certain desirable properties and (2) development of special higher-level diagrams to deal with scale-up issues of concern on large projects. There have also been a number of collateral improvements aimed at clarifying the presentation of certain concepts and at increasing the traceability of elements of the graphic models. For practitioners who have been exposed to OOA through our consulting practice, training courses, or publications, here is a summary of what is new in "OOA91."

Information Models. Objects are now assigned key letters (in addition to their object numbers) to make it easier to correlate various elements of the models. A relationship-numbering convention has been added to support correlation of model elements and to increase understandability of the graphical representation of the information model. We have also abandoned the correlation table as an entity of the formalism. This was originally seen as a pedagogical device aimed at facilitating understanding of the associative object, but students in our training courses have made it clear that this intellectual stepping stone is both unnecessary and distracting. We have therefore merged the two concepts into the more general associative object.

State models. The monitor state model, previously used to formalize dynamics of a competitive relationship, has been generalized, and appears in OOA91 as a special case of the more general Assigner state model. The matter of lifecycles for subtype and supertype objects has been clarified. At the request of our real-time clients, the Timer object has been promoted to become an element of the formalism, and is no longer seen as a user-supplied object. And finally, an alternative convention for labeling events has been developed; while this is a minor matter, we believe that the new destination-based labeling (see Chapter 3) makes it much easier to keep track of the events.

Process models. Most of the significant changes have occurred in the process modeling step. Guidelines have been formulated for casting the actions into separate processes, for naming the processes, and for describing them. The order of process execution is now captured on the action data flow diagrams, and conditional outputs are shown explicitly. Finally, a long-standing (and semantically significant) problem with data flow diagrams has been addressed: How to label a data flow between two processes that have entirely different perspectives on the meaning of the data.

What is to Come

For the past several years, we have been working on methods for transforming OOA models into designs of various types. This work, known as Recursive Design (RD), has now come to fruition. While a complete exposition is beyond the scope of this book, a particular object-oriented example is provided in the final chapter. Please note that the design presented is not the only possible solution: one of the strengths of RD is that it allows the engineer a wide range of choice and control over the type of design produced.

Acknowledgements

This book has been greatly enhanced by numerous ideas and suggestions from our colleagues, clients, and friends. On the technical front, we are deeply indebted to: Rob Burnside (Abbott Critical Care) for insightful observations on the various ways we, as software engineers, view time; Yue Min Wong (FMC Corporation) for presenting us with the "session and segment" problem which, at the time, strained our understanding of object layering, and subsequently contributed to a better view; Christian Fortunel (also of FMC Corporation) for the simple and most effective suggestion of numbering relationships on the information model; Jonathan Sandoe (Ampex Corporation) for investigation of lifecycle forms for subtypes and supertypes; and Bill Greiman (Lawrence Berkeley Laboratory) for the conceptualization of the very powerful and reusable pipe path object as shown in Chapter 5. We are also grateful to Bill and to Deborah Ohlsen and Leon Starr for work on the original version of Project Technology's training course on state and process modeling: many of their careful presentations and examples remain at the core of OOA as it stands today. Also to Stan Levine (FATDS Program, Fort Monmouth) for encouragement with (and funding for) the 2167A work reported in Appendix B; to Steve Lewis (Lawrence Berkeley Laboratory) for the nifty little performance monitoring scheme described in Chapter 7, and to Rick Hill (Sandia National Laboratory) for clarification of the concept of accessors, for the terms active and passive as used in Chapter 9, and for assistance with OODLE.

We are also delighted to acknowledge the contributions of Klancy de Nevers (Eyring Research) for first insisting that we provide guidance for our 2167A clients and then for her contributions to that effort; Peter DiPrete (NEC America) for the term parameter line as used in OODLE; Alan Hecht (Mesa Systems Guild) for constructive and helpful review of the OODLE paper, and to both Alan and Dave Fortin (also of Mesa) for numerous practical suggestions on the use of OODLE with CASE.

Closer to home, we are delighted to recognize the many contributions of the Project Technology instructors and consultants who have participated in the development and refinement of OOA and RD. We particularly want to thank our long-time friend and colleague, Wayne Hywari, for his collaboration on OODLE and for research on various object-oriented architectures; Neil Lang, the current custodian of the OOA91 rules, for clarifying the concept of the Assigner model and for developing consistent conventions for dealing with Assigner events; and Phil Ryals, for development of the C++ templates shown in Chapter 9.

From the perspective of actually making the book, we are indebted to (in chronological order): First, Paul Becker, our acquisitions editor at Prentice Hall, who cajoled, encouraged and berated us (charmingly) in a patient effort to extract a manuscript from two somewhat harried authors; to Kathleen Gadway, our book designer, whose artistry with type and space continues to delight us; and especially to Sharon Hiromoto (Project Technology) who produced the entire book — including all 148 figures — in camera-ready form for printing. We are also grateful to Phil Ryals, now in his role as PostScript wizard extraordinaire, for diagnosis and cure of incompatibilities in the publishing software that baffled even the software suppliers, and finally to Harriet Tellem, our production editor at Prentice Hall, who executed the myriads of mysterious coordinations required to put these pages between covers and into your hands.

Finally, very special thanks to Neil Davenport, Beth Breedlove, and the entire PT staff for taking on many additional operational responsibilities so that we could have time for writing. Without their support, this project could well have turned out to be OOA2001.

Sally Shlaer
Stephen J. Mellor

Berkeley, California

Overview of
Object-Oriented Analysis

This chapter provides a quick introduction to Object-Oriented Analysis, or OOA. We visit most of the major graphical models used in this method in the order in which they are most commonly developed. The chapter closes with a guide to the remainder of the book.

1.1 Setting Up for the Analysis

In building a typical large software system, the analyst generally has to deal with a number of distinctly different subject matters, or ***domains***. Each domain can be thought of as a separate world inhabited by its own conceptual entities, or objects. Hence, in an Automated Railroad Management System, a Railroad Operations domain is concerned with trains, tracks and the like, while a User Interface domain is involved with windows, displays, and icons.

Each domain can exist more or less independently of the others:

- A railroad can exist without screens or windows.
- Windows and icons can exist without trains.

The domains are depicted on a domain chart, as shown in Figure 1.1.1.

1

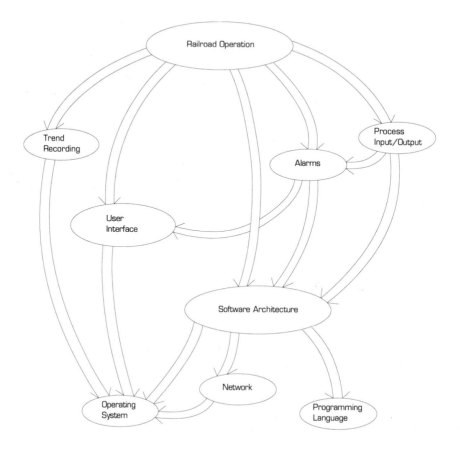

Figure 1.1.1: Domain chart for the Automated Railroad Management
System. Each domain is represented as an oval. A
connection between two domains indicates that the higher
domain will make use of facilities provided by
the lower domain in the implemented system.

Some domains are small enough to be analyzed as a whole, while others contain
so many objects as to be unmanageable. Large domains are therefore partitioned
into **subsystems**, as depicted in the project matrix of Figure 1.1.2.

Once the system has been partitioned into domains and subsystems, we are
ready to embark on the analysis proper. Each subsystem (or small domain) is
analyzed separately in three steps: information modeling, state modeling, and
process modeling. These steps are described in the next sections.

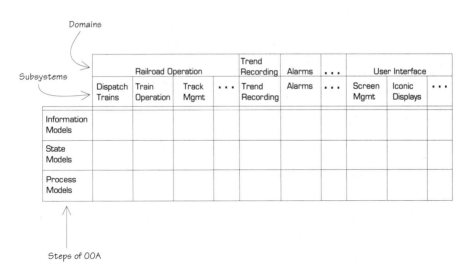

Figure 1.1.2: Project matrix for the Automated Railroad Management System. The boxes represent units of work to be accomplished during analysis.

1.2 Information Models

The goal of the information modeling step is to identify the conceptual entities, or **objects**, making up the subsystem under analysis. The objects are depicted on an information model (Figure 1.2.1) together with their characteristics, or **attributes**. **Relationships** that pertain between objects are represented on the graphic model as connections between the objects.

A complete description or definition of each object, attribute, and relationship must be prepared as documentation for the graphic model.

1.3 State Models

Now that the objects and relationships have been identified, we turn to the investigation of their behavior over time. In OOA, each object and relationship may have a lifecycle — an orderly pattern of behavior. For example, a train that is traveling along the tracks must slow down as it enters a station. Having arrived at the platform, the train must stop before opening its doors. Later, the

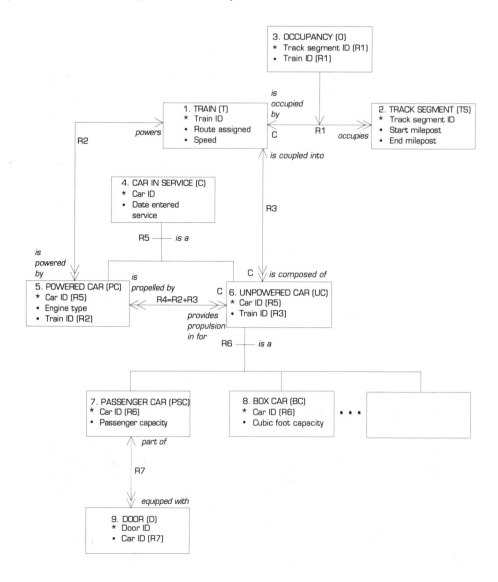

Figure 1.2.1: Partial information model for the Train Operation subsystem. A typical information model has between 20 and 60 objects.

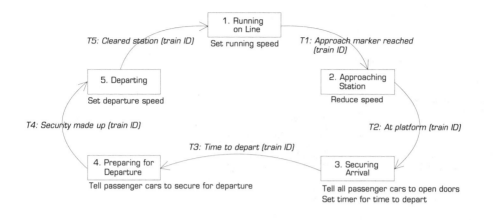

Figure 1.3.1: State model for the Train object.

train can prepare to depart by ringing bells or otherwise signaling the passengers that departure is imminent. Finally, the doors must be closed before the train pulls out of the station.

Such a lifecycle is formalized in a state model: a set of states and events. A **state** represents a situation or condition of the object during which certain physical laws, rules, and policies apply. An **event** represents an incident that causes the object to move from one state to another.

A separate state model is built for every object and relationship that has interesting dynamic behavior. A state model for the train object is shown in Figure 1.3.1. Note that some activity has been associated with each state. This activity, properly termed an **action**, occurs when the object arrives in the state.

In order to achieve coordinated behavior between the various objects, the state models are allowed to communicate with one another via events: the train state model can generate an event to the door to tell it to open. Such communication is represented on the object communication model (Figure 1.3.2). A separate object communication model is built for each subsystem.

Once the object communication models have been developed for all the subsystems in a domain, a subsystem communication model can be drawn to depict event communication between the subsystems. A subsystem communication model is shown in Figure 1.3.3.

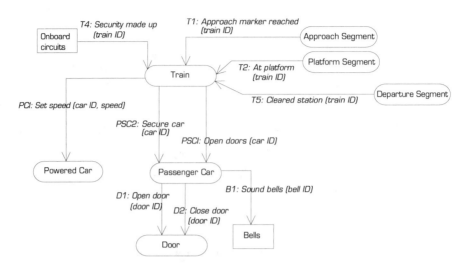

Figure 1.3.2: Partial object communication model for the Train
Operation subsystem.

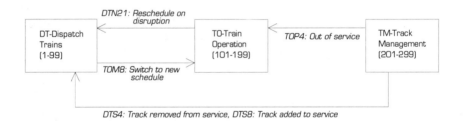

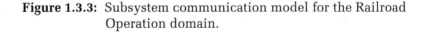

Figure 1.3.3: Subsystem communication model for the Railroad
Operation domain.

1.4 Process Models

All the processing in the system is contained in the actions of the state models.
Each action is now defined in terms of processes and object data stores, where
a process is a fundamental unit of operation and an object data store corresponds
to the data (attributes) of an object on the information model. Each

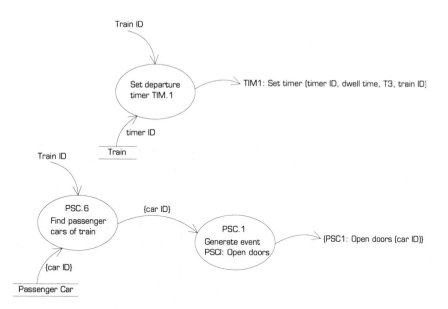

Figure 1.4.1: Action data flow diagram for the Securing Arrival
state of the Train object.

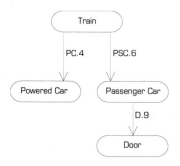

Figure 1.4.2: Partial object access model for the Train
Operation subsystem.

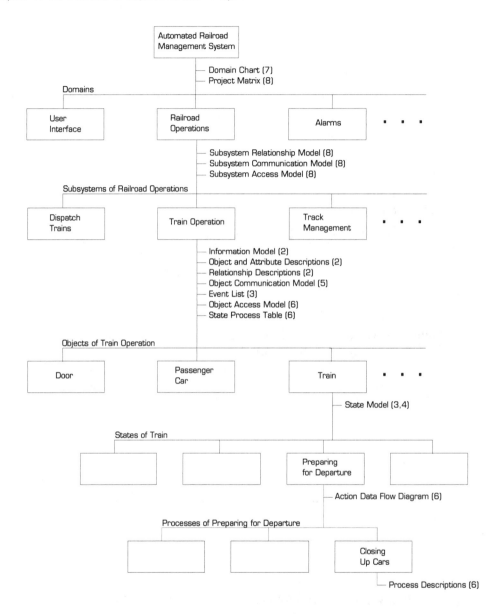

Figure 1.5.1: The OOA work products for the Automated Railroad Management System. Each work product has been annotated with the chapter number in which it is described in detail.

action is depicted graphically in an action data flow diagram (ADFD), as shown in Figure 1.4.1. Note that a separate ADFD is produced for each action of each state model.

Processes of an action may access both the data of the object in whose state model they are embedded as well as the data of other objects. A view of such interobject data access is provided by the object access model, as shown in Figure 1.4.2.

Finally, process descriptions are developed to document the details of any complex processes found on the ADFDs.

1.5 The Work Products of OOA

Figure 1.5.1 provides an information map of the work products of OOA. In this figure we see that a domain chart and a project matrix are produced for the entire system. A subsystem communication model is produced for each domain in order to depict the event communication between the various subsystems within the domain. The majority of the work products of OOA are placed at the subsystem level: an information model, an object communication model, an object access model and supporting tables, descriptions, and lists are produced for each subsystem. Below the subsystem lie the objects that make it up; A state model is produced for each object and relationship that has interesting dynamic behavior. The actions of each state model provide the next level; an action data flow diagram is produced for each state of each state model. Finally, a process description is produced for each complex process of the action.

1.6 Preview

We start out at the subsystem level in Chapter 2, which provides a summary of information modeling concepts. In Chapter 3, we discuss in detail how to formalize the lifecycle of each object that was identified in the information model. Chapter 4 takes up the subject of dynamic relationships. In Chapter 5, we present the object communication model together with techniques for understanding and describing the dynamics of the entire subsystem. Chapter 6 discusses the action data flow diagrams and the object access model. Chapters 7 and 8 present domains and subsystems. Finally, in Chapter 9 we look at one approach for deriving an object-oriented design from the OOA models.

2
Information Modeling Concepts

This chapter provides a short review of information modeling concepts, terminology, and notation. For a more thorough presentation, including examples, guidelines, quality criteria and rationale, see reference [1].

2.1 Objects

Concept of an Object

We start out with a definition. In OOA,

An *object* is an abstraction of a set of real-world things such that

- all the things in the set—the instances—have the same characteristics, and

- all instances are subject to and conform to the same set of rules and policies.

Like Things   **Object**

ABSTRACTED

AIRPLANE
- * Airplane ID
- • Flight number
- • Altitude
- • Wingspan

Each object in the model must be provided with a unique and meaningful name as well as a unique key letter: a short form of the object's name that can be used to correlate other elements of the OOA model with the object. In a sizeable model, the objects should also be numbered for purposes of organizing the documentation.

An object in OOA represents a single *typical* but *unspecified instance* of something in the real world—any airplane, I don't care which one, as long as it is typical. The object-oriented analyst distinguishes this concept from that of a *specified instance*: Airplane number N2713A, Air Force One, or The Spirit of St. Louis, for example.

There is no special term in OOA for the collection of existing instances of an object.*

Identifying Objects

Objects are identified by considering what the conceptual entities, or "things," are in the problem being analyzed. Certain problems tend to yield objects that have a very physical nature: in the operation of an airport, you would likely find objects such as Airplane, Runway, and Control Tower. Other problems yield more abstract objects: a communications system might have objects such as Outgoing Data Frame Message or Incoming Acknowledgment Message.

While an object can be abstracted from virtually anything, most objects we encounter fall into the following categories:

- tangible objects
- roles
- incidents
- interactions
- specifications

---

*The reader is advised to approach the object-oriented literature with some caution, since terminology varies somewhat from author to author and programming language to programming language. The collection of existing instances is usually called a class. The behavior of a typical unspecified instance may also be incorporated in "class"; alternatively, "object type" and "object" are sometimes used for this concept. A specified (or typical unspecified) instance is referred to variously as object, object instance, and instance.

Tangible objects are abstractions of the actual existence of some thing in the physical world.

In a juice bottling plant: Pipe, Pump, Valve, Tank
In a shipping application: Package, Delivery Vehicle

Roles are abstractions of the purpose or assignment of a person, piece of equipment, or organization.

In a university: Student, Instructor, Advisor
In a chemical plant: Isolation Valve, Tank Inlet Valve
In county government: Taxpayer, Jury Member, Voter

An *incident* is an abstraction of some happening or occurrence.

Accident (in an insurance application)
Earthquake
Election
Delivery (by a shipping company)

Interactions are objects that result from associations between other objects.

Connection: the meeting of two pipes
Contract: an agreement between two parties
Intersection: the place where two or more streets meet

Specification objects are used to represent rules, standards, or quality criteria (as opposed to the tangible object or role that meets these standards).

A Recipe represents the rules for making a certain quantity of a certain food (as opposed to the batch of food prepared according to the recipe).

A Compound represents the composition of a chemical (but not a particular sample of that compound).

Object Descriptions

A description must be provided for each object. The description is a short informative statement that allows us to tell with certainty whether a real-world thing is or is not an instance of the object at hand. The object description should concentrate on the basis for abstraction, explaining exactly in what manner the real-world things are alike.

Object Description (Meter Reader): A meter reader is a State Electric employee who (1) is qualified to read the values displayed on electricity meters and (2) is currently assigned to this job. Anyone who has ever attended a training session in meter reading procedures is regarded as qualified to read meters.

In preparing object descriptions, we must often refer to real-world entities as well as to formal objects in the model. To help the reader distinguish between these two possibilities, we use an initial capital letter on all words in the name of an object and lowercase letters when referring to instances in the real world.

2.2 Attributes

Concept of an Attribute

Things in the real world have characteristics, such as height, temperature, registration number, or location. Each separate characteristic that is common to all possible instances of the object is abstracted as a separate attribute.

Definition. An *attribute* is an abstraction of a single characteristic possessed by all entities that were themselves abstracted as an object.

Each attribute is provided with a name unique within the object.

To refer to an attribute, write <object name>.<attribute name>, as in

Airplane.Wingspan
Cat.Weight
Valve.Open/Closed Status

Domains and Attribute Values

For any specified instance, an attribute can take on a value. For example, suppose that we have a Cat object with attributes Name, Sex, Weight, Color Scheme, Temperament. Then

SALLY'S CAT
Name: Gruesome
Sex: male
Weight: 15.75 lb
Color Scheme: brown tabby
Temperament: incredibly lazy

STEVE'S CAT
Name: PacMan
Sex: female
Weight: 9.25 lb
Color Scheme: tortoise shell
Temperament: lusty wench

The range of legal values that an attribute can take on is called its *domain*. The domain must be specified for each attribute; how this is done is explained in a subsequent section.

Identifiers

An *identifier* is a set of one or more attributes whose values uniquely distinguish each instance of an object.

Using the cat example, the Name attribute is a satisfactory identifier for the Cat object as long as we have a policy of giving each cat its own unique name. However, the Weight attribute cannot be an identifier, since it is possible to have two cats with the same weight.

Every object must have an identifier. An object may have several identifiers, each composed of one or more attributes. For example, an Airport object may have attributes

    Airport Code
    Latitude
    Longitude
    City
    Number of Passenger Gates

The Airport Code attribute is an identifier of the Airport object, and the combination of Latitude and Longitude is another identifier of Airport.

If an object has multiple identifiers, one such identifier is chosen as the *preferred identifier*.

Representation

An object can be represented together with its attributes in several different ways. In the graphical representation (see Figure 2.2.1), an object is represented by a box containing the name, number and key letter of the object and the names of the attributes. Attributes that make up the preferred identifier of the object are marked with an asterisk at the left side of the attribute name. All other attributes are set off with a dot or some other convenient symbol.

In an equivalent textual representation, the preferred identifier is underlined:

    Cat (Name, Sex, Weight, Color Scheme, Temperament)

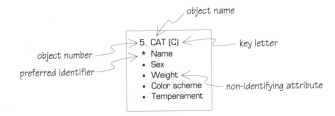

Figure 2.2.1: Graphical representation of the Cat object.

Table Interpretation

An object on the information model can be interpreted as a table, as in Figure 2.2.2. In this interpretation, each instance of the object is a row in the table. The row is filled out with attribute values appropriate for each instance.

We find the table interpretation useful for constructing examples and for making presentations to nontechnical audiences. Note that the table is not intended as a statement of the data structure to be used in implementation: the canny designer will recognize that numerous equivalent data structures may be appropriate alternatives in different situations.

Types of Attributes

Attributes can be classified into three different types:

- descriptive attributes
- naming attributes
- referential attributes

Descriptive attributes provide facts intrinsic to each instance of the object.

    Account.Balance
    Power Supply.Polarity
    Cat.Weight

If the value of a descriptive attribute changes, it means only that some aspect of an instance has changed, but the instance is still the same instance. For

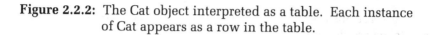

Cat				
Name	Sex	Weight	Color Scheme	Temperament
Gruesome	M	15.75	brown tabby	incredibly lazy
PacMan	F	9.25	tortoise shell	lusty wench
Lappi	F	8	tortoise shell	prissy
Munchi	M	9.75	orange & white	affectionate
Mindy	F	7	tortoise shell	spinsterish
Smudge	F	8.75	calico	shy
Dipper	F	8.25	calico	career-oriented
Fanbelt	M	10.5	siamese	mellow
Deckard	M	10.25	black	floppy

Figure 2.2.2: The Cat object interpreted as a table. Each instance of Cat appears as a row in the table.

example, if PacMan gains a pound, a fact about this cat has changed, but she is still the same cat.

Naming attributes are used to name or label instances. Names are typically somewhat arbitrary.

Account.Number
Shipment.Waybill Number
Flight.Number

Naming attributes are frequently (but not always) used as an identifier or as part of an identifier.

If the value of a naming attribute changes, it means only that a new name has been given to exactly the same instance. Changing PacMan's name to DingBat does not change the cat in any way.

Referential attributes are used to tie an instance of one object to an instance of another.

Cat.Owner Name indicates which person owns this cat.

Account.Customer ID indicates which customer is the owner of this account.

Magnet.Power Supply indicates which power supply is being used to power this magnet.

If the value of a referential attribute changes, it means that different instances are now being associated. If we change the value of Magnet.Power Supply from PS10 to PS12, we indicate that the magnet is now being powered by power supply PS12.

Describing Attributes and Domains

Each attribute requires an attribute description: a few-sentence description that tells what characteristic is being captured in the attribute. The domain of each attribute must also be described.

These descriptions are written somewhat differently depending on the type of attribute we are dealing with.

Descriptive attributes. The attribute description must state the real-world characteristic being abstracted as an attribute. It may also explain how the characteristic is measured or determined and, if it is not entirely obvious, why the characteristic is pertinent to the definition of the object.

The domain description may be given by:

- enumeration of all the possible values that the attribute may take on.
- citation of a document that lists the possible values.
- the statement of a rule that determines which values are permitted.
- the statement of a range of possible values.

Naming attributes. An attribute description for a naming attribute states the form of the name (if the form is relevant), the organization that assigns the name (again, if relevant), and the extent to which the name may be used as a part of the identifier. If the attribute description says as much as can be said about the legal values for the naming attribute, the domain is specified by

Domain: See attribute description or
Domain: See above (when preceded by the attribute description).

Employee	Mail Stop	Office Number
Al Aardvark	17	B422
Betty Baer	3	I604
Celeste Caribou	41	D296
		B426

Owner	Model	Manufacturer	License #
Brown	Sedan	Ford	16923A
Green	Van	Chevrolet	23004C
Jones	Collie		29-A-101

NOT OK   NOT OK

Figure 2.2.3: Two violations of the first rule of attribution.

Alternatively, the domain of a naming attribute can be specified by enumeration or citation.

Referential attributes. The attribute description for a referential attribute must indicate the real-world association being captured by the attribute. For example, the attribute Magnet.Power Supply can be described as "The name of the power supply currently being used to power this magnet."

The value that a referential attribute may take on will always be the same as the value for some attribute acting as an identifier for the associated object. Consequently, the domain description is always given by the phrase "Same as <name of identifying attribute of associated object>", as in

Attribute: Magnet.Power Supply
Description: . . .
Domain: Same as Power Supply.Power Supply ID

Rules of Attribution

The information model is based on the relational model of data: a view of data that emphasizes its meaning [2, 3]. The relational model is defined in certain statements about the forms we use in the information model and the meaning we imply when we assign an attribute to an object.

First Rule: One instance of an object has exactly one value for each attribute at any given time.

Pump		
Pump ID	Manufacturer Model	On/Off Status
P101	Acme 126	on
P203	Zenith 17A3	off
•••	•••	•••

Figure 2.2.4: A possible violation of the second rule.

In the table interpretation of an object, this rule requires that there be one and only one data element at each row-column intersection. It forbids a table with a "repeating group" structure as well as a table with holes (Figure 2.2.3).

Second Rule: An attribute must contain no internal structure.

The second rule implies that if you define an object as in Figure 2.2.4, you mean to think of Manufacturer and Model as a single characteristic, and that you can't break up "Acme 126" to find out that pump P101 was made by Acme.

Third Rule: When an object has a compound identifier—that is, one made up of two or more attributes—every attribute that is not part of the identifier represents a characteristic of the *entire object*, not a characteristic of something that would be identified by a part of the identifier.

The third rule implies that if you define an object Juice Transfer

> Juice Transfer (<u>Storage Tank ID</u>, <u>Cooking Tank ID</u>, Gallons, Planned Time of Transfer),

the Juice Transfer.Gallons attribute means the number of gallons transferred from the storage tank to the cooking tank, and not the number of gallons in either the storage tank or the cooking tank.

Fourth Rule: Each attribute that is not a part of an identifier represents a characteristic of the instance named by the identifier and not a characteristic of some other nonidentifier attribute.

According to the fourth rule, if you define an object

> Batch (<u>Batch ID</u>, Recipe ID, Gallons, Cooking Time),

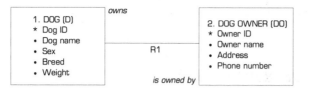

Figure 2.3.1: Graphical representation of the relationship Dog Owner OWNS Dog / Dog IS OWNED BY Dog Owner.

the attribute Batch.Cooking Time must represent the actual time the batch was cooked, and not the cooking time specified by the recipe.

2.3 Relationships

Concept of a Relationship

Associations exist between different kinds of things in the real world.

A *relationship* is an abstraction of a set of associations that hold systematically between different kinds of things in the real world.

The real-world things that participate in the association must themselves be abstracted as objects.

Every relationship in the model is given a pair of names that describe the relationship from the perspective of each of the participating objects.

Dog Owner OWNS Dog
Dog IS OWNED BY Dog Owner

Note that this is a single relationship.

Every relationship is given a unique identifier of the form R1, R2, and so on.

Representation

A relationship is represented graphically by a line between the associated objects (Figure 2.3.1). The line is annotated with the relationship's identifier.

The names of the relationship are placed at each end of the relationship line as shown in the figure.

Unconditional Relationships

There are three fundamental forms for a relationship: one-to-one, one-to-many, and many-to-many. These fundamental forms are called the *unconditional forms* because every instance of both objects is required to participate in the relationship.

A *one-to-one relationship* exists when a single instance of an object is associated with a single instance of another.

A *one-to-many relationship* exists when a single instance of an object is associated with one or more instances of another, and each instance of the second object is associated with just one instance of the first.

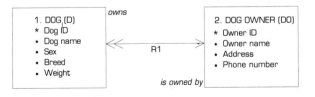

A *many-to-many relationship* exists when a single instance of an object is associated with one or more instances of another, and each instance of the second object is associated with one or more instances of the first.

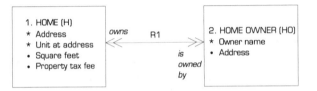

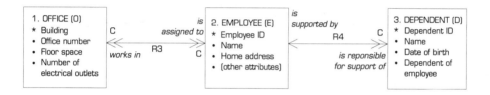

Figure 2.3.2: Conditional relationships.

The terms one-to-one, one-to-many, and many-to-many are statements of the *multiplicity* of a relationship. Note that the multiplicity is indicated graphically, with a single arrowhead meaning "one instance" and a double arrowhead meaning "one or more instances."

Conditional Forms

In the unconditional relationships discussed above, every instance of the objects was required to participate in the relationship. In a conditional relationship there can be instances of the objects that do not participate. This situation is represented by placing a "c" (for "conditional") next to the relationship phrase that is sometimes true. The relationship R4 in Figure 2.3.2 is conditional on one side only since there can be employees with no dependents, but there cannot be a dependent without an associated employee.

If the relationship is conditional on both sides—meaning that there can be instances of both objects that do not participate in the relationship—the relationship is termed *biconditional*. In this case, the "c" marker is placed on both relationship phrases. Relationship R3 in Figure 2.3.2 is biconditional since some employees are not assigned to any office and some offices are not assigned to any employee.

Including both the conditional and unconditional forms, there are ten distinct forms for relationships involving two objects. The forms are summarized in Figure 2.3.3.

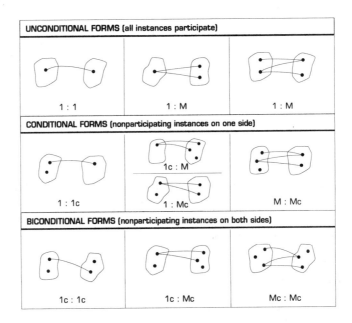

Figure 2.3.3: The ten forms of a relationship.

Relationship Descriptions

All relationships require a description. The description must provide:

- the identifier of the relationship
- a statement of the names of the relationship from the point of view of each participating object
- the form of the relationship (its multiplicity and conditionality)
- a statement of the basis of abstraction
- a statement of how the relationship has been formalized (a subject to be discussed in the next section).

2.4   Relationship Formalization

The purpose of a relationship is to allow us to state which instances of one object are associated with which instances of another. This is accomplished by

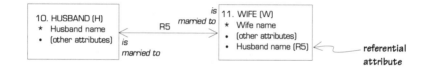

Figure 2.4.1: Formalizing a one-to-one relationship with
referential attributes.

placing referential attributes in appropriate objects on the model. When this has
been done, the relationship is said to have been formalized in data.

To formalize a one-to-one relationship, referential attributes may be added to
either object (but not both). The referential attributes are tagged with the
relationship's identifier, as in Figure 2.4.1.

In a one-to-many relationship, referential attributes must be added to the object
on the "many" side (see Figure 2.4.2), since placing such a referential attribute
on the "one" side would violate the third rule of attribution.

To formalize a many-to-many relationship, create an *associative object*—a
separate object that contains references to the identifiers of each of the participating instances (Figure 2.4.3). The associative object is then treated as

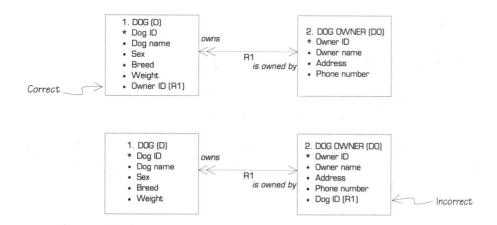

Figure 2.4.2: Correct and incorrect formalization of a
one-to-many relationship.

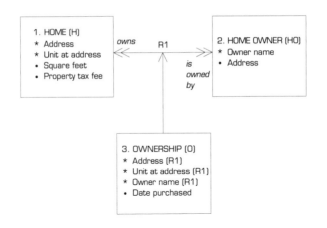

Figure 2.4.3: Formalizing a many-to-many relationship by means of an associative object.

an object in its own right, with a name, number, key letter and object description. Like any other object, the associative object may have additional attributes and may participate in relationships with other objects.

An associative object may be used to formalize any relationship, not only a many-to-many relationship. As we will see in Chapter 4, a relationship with dynamic behavior must be formalized by means of an associative object.

2.5 Composition of Relationships

Some relationships come about as a necessary consequence of the existence of other relationships. This will be demonstrated through an example.

Consider the case of University A. At this institution, each student is required to declare a single major field of studies. The field of studies must be represented by a department that specializes in the subject. Each department is staffed with professors.

At University A, a student selects a professor to be his or her advisor throughout the course of study. The professor may be from any department, so a student majoring in mathematics can have as advisor a professor of physics. The information model for University A appears in Figure 2.5.1.

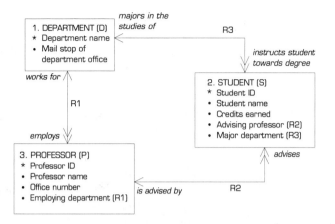

Figure 2.5.1: The information model for University A. Relationships R1, R2 and R3 are formed independently of one another.

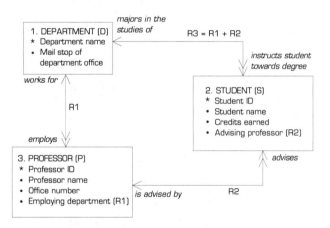

Figure 2.5.2: The information model for University B. Relationship R3 is the logical consequence of relationships R1 and R2.

Figure 2.6.1: Objects with attributes in common.

Now consider University B. The policies at B are the same as at A, except that a student is required to select a professor from his or her major department. The information model at University B (Figure 2.5.2) is slightly different, since the R3 relationship is the logical consequence of relationships R1 and R2: If a student is advised by a professor, the student must necessarily be majoring in the studies of the professor's department.

Such a relationship is said to have been formed by composition (as in composition of functions in mathematics). A relationship formed by composition cannot be formalized in referential attributes, since the connection between the instances (students and departments, in this case) is already given by the connections between the students and professors, and then between the professors and their departments.

A relationship formed by composition is annotated on the model as R3 = R1 + R2, meaning that R3 is the logical consequence of R1 and R2.

2.6 Subtypes and Supertypes

In many problems you will find distinct specialized objects that have certain attributes in common (Figure 2.6.1). In this case, we can abstract a more general object to represent the characteristics shared by the original specialized objects. These objects are related through a subtype-supertype relationship as shown in Figure 2.6.2. The bar across the relationship line is placed next to the more general, or supertype, object.

Attributes that are common to all the subtype objects are placed in the supertype object. The subtype objects will also have additional attributes to support the more specialized abstractions represented by each subtype.

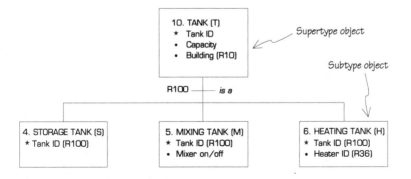

Figure 2.6.2: Subtype and supertype objects formed from objects with attributes in common.

In a subtype-supertype construct, one real-world instance is represented by the combination of an instance of the supertype and an instance of exactly one subtype. In contrast to some object-oriented programming languages, OOA does not permit creating an instance of the supertype without creating an instance of one subtype, and vice versa.*

The subtype-supertype construct can be drawn on successively in the same problem, as shown in Figure 2.6.3.

---

*A supertype object is therefore analogous to a parent abstract class in Smalltalk and the parent deferred class in Eiffel. Subtype objects are analogous to child classes in virtually all object-oriented programming languages.

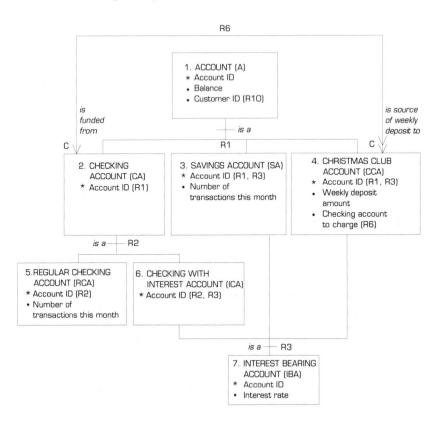

Figure 2.6.3: An object can participate in multiple subtype-supertype constructs.

2.7 Work Products

Three work products are developed for the information model of a subsystem:

Information Structure Diagram. The information structure diagram is a graphic representation of the information model. This drawing is sometimes referred to as an Entity-Relationship Diagram or simply as the Information Model.

Object and Attribute Descriptions. The Object and Attribute Description document lists each object and attribute in the model and provides an organized collection of the object, attribute, and domain descriptions.

Relationship Descriptions. The Relationship Description document lists each relationship of the model together with its relationship description.

References

[1] Sally Shlaer and Stephen J. Mellor, *Object-Oriented Systems Analysis: Modeling the World in Data,* Prentice Hall, Englewood Cliffs, N.J., 1988.

[2] E. F. Codd, "A Relational Model of Data for Large Shared Data Banks," *Communications of the ACM*, Vol. 13, No. 6, June 1970.

[3] C. J. Date, *An Introduction to Database Systems*, Addison-Wesley, Reading, Mass., 1977.

3

Lifecycles of Objects

This chapter describes how to formalize the dynamic behavior of objects in terms of state models.

3.1 Behavior Patterns in the Real World

When we turn to consider the dynamic behavior of things in the real world, we observe that things in the world generally have a lifetime. Often something is created or comes into existence, progresses through certain stages of its existence, and then dies or vanishes. A classic example is that of the light bulb: After having been manufactured, the light bulb is installed in a socket where it is then alternately lit and unlit. From time to time the light bulb may be moved from one light socket to another; eventually the light bulb breaks and is discarded. This same simple but interesting pattern of dynamic behavior is followed by all light bulbs throughout their lifetimes.

We offer the following general observations regarding behavior patterns for different things in the real world:

- Many things go through various stages during their lifetimes. The airplane of Figure 3.1.1 can be parked at a gate, taxiing to the runway, flying, and so forth.

- The order in which a thing progresses through its stages forms a pattern characteristic of the kind of thing it is.

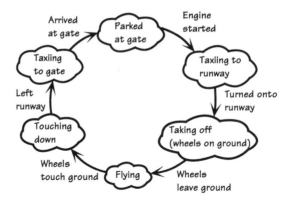

Figure 3.1.1: Behavior pattern of an airplane.

- A real-world thing is in exactly one stage of its behavior pattern at any given time. An airplane cannot be parked at a gate and taking off at the same time.

- Things progress from one stage to another abruptly, in part because of how we choose to define or perceive stages. We define flying to be the stage of the airplane's behavior when the wheels are off the ground.

- In a behavior pattern, not all progressions between stages are allowed. Some progressions are forbidden by laws of physics, some by statute, and so forth. The laws of physics prevent an airplane from progressing directly from flying to parked at a gate.

- There are incidents in the real world that cause things to progress (or indicate that they have progressed) between stages. Starting the airplane's motor causes the airplane to progress from parked at a gate to taxiing to runway.

3.2 Lifecycles and the State Transition Diagram

Recall the definition of an object:

An object is an abstraction of a set of real-world things such that

- all of the real-world things in the set—the instances—have the same characteristics, and

- all instances are subject to and conform to the same rules.

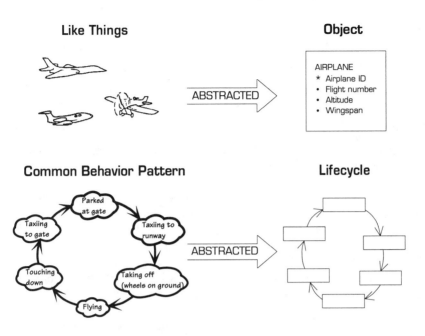

Figure 3.2.1: When we abstract like things to produce an object, we also abstract their common behavior pattern to produce the lifecycle of a typical unspecified instance.

Since all instances of the object must follow the same rules of behavior, when we abstract a group of like things to produce an object, we also abstract their common behavior pattern into a lifecycle typical of the object, as indicated in Figure 3.2.1. The lifecycle provides a formal description of the behavior pattern shared by all the instances.

Lifecycles as State Models

A lifecycle is expressed as a state model. Two forms of state models are commonly used in analysis; in OOA, we use the Moore form [1]. A Moore state model is composed of:

- A set of *states*. Each state represents a stage in the lifecycle of a typical instance of the object.

- A set of *events*. Each event represents an incident or indication that a progression is happening.

- Transition rules (or *transitions*, for short). A transition rule specifies what new state is achieved when an instance in a given state receives a particular event.

- *Actions.* An action is an activity or operation that must be accomplished when an instance arrives in a state. One action is associated with each state.

The state model can be represented in a diagrammatic form known as a state transition diagram, as illustrated by the next example.

Example. Suppose we are going to build a compact, inexpensive microwave oven, the One-minute Microwaver. The product concept includes the following points:

1. There is a single control button available for the user of the oven. If the oven door is closed and you push the button, the oven will cook (that is, energize the power tube) for 1 minute.

2. If you push the button at any time when the oven is cooking, you get an additional minute of cooking time. That is, if you have 40 seconds more cooking time to go and you push the button twice, you are set to cook for 2 minutes and 40 seconds.

3. Pushing the button when the door is open has no effect.

4. There is a light inside the oven. Any time the oven is cooking, the light must be turned on (so that you can peer through the window in the oven's door and see if your food is boiling over). Any time the door is open, the light must be on (so that you can see your food or so you have enough light to clean the oven).

5. You can stop the cooking by opening the door.

6. If you close the door, the light goes out. This is the normal configuration when someone has just placed food inside the oven but has not yet pushed the control button.

7. If the oven times out (cooks until the desired preset time), it turns off both the power tube and the light. It then emits a warning beep to tell you that the food is ready.

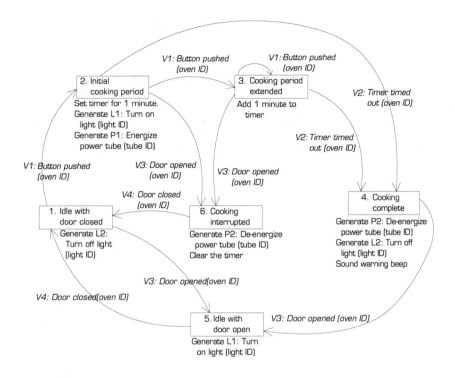

Figure 3.2.2: State model for the one-minute microwave oven.

In this problem there are several pertinent incidents that affect the operation of the oven:

opening the door
closing the door
pushing the control button
completion of the prescribed cooking interval

These incidents are abstracted as events.

A state transition diagram (STD) for the 1-minute microwave oven is shown in Figure 3.2.2. The states are represented by boxes, each labeled with an appropriate name for the state. The transitions are shown by arcs connecting two states. Each transition is labeled with the event that causes the transition. The action associated with a state is described under the state box.

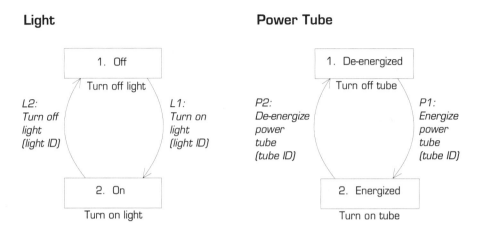

Figure 3.2.3: State models for the power tube and light.

Coordination of Lifecycles

Lifecycles of different objects are frequently coordinated with one another. For example, in the case of the microwave oven, the power tube and light have lifecycles that are closely linked to the state of the oven itself (Figure 3.2.3). The state model of the oven generates the energize and de-energize events that cause the power tube to move through its state model. Similarly, the oven generates events to tell the light to turn on and off.

State Models vs. State Machines

Although all instances of an object share the same state model, it is sometimes necessary to distinguish between the state model as executed by one instance (power tube 92, say) and the state model as executed by another (power tube 256). We use the term *state machine* to refer to the execution of a state model by a particular instance. Alternatively, you can think of a state machine as a private copy of the state model that is executed by a single instance (Figure 3.2.4).

3.3 States

A *state* represents a condition of the object in which a defined set of rules, policies, regulations, and physical laws applies. The states are shown as boxes on the STD.

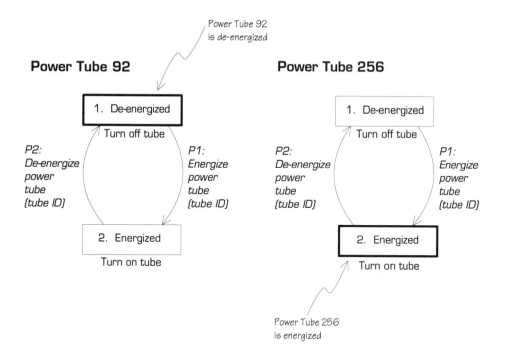

Figure 3.2.4: State machines for power tubes 92 and 256.

State Names and Numbers

Each state is given a name that is unique within this state model. The state boxes on the STD are labeled with the names of the states.

Each state is also given a number, again unique within the state model. The state numbers are primarily used in a tabular representation of the state model (to be described in Section 3.6), and do not necessarily prescribe the order in which an instance would occupy the states. Note that the state numbers appear on the STD.

Creation State

Some state models have one or more states in which an instance first comes into existence. Such states are known as *creation states*. A creation state is shown on the STD as a box in the normal manner. However, a transition into a creation state is depicted as a transition from no state, as shown in Figure 3.3.1.

Account

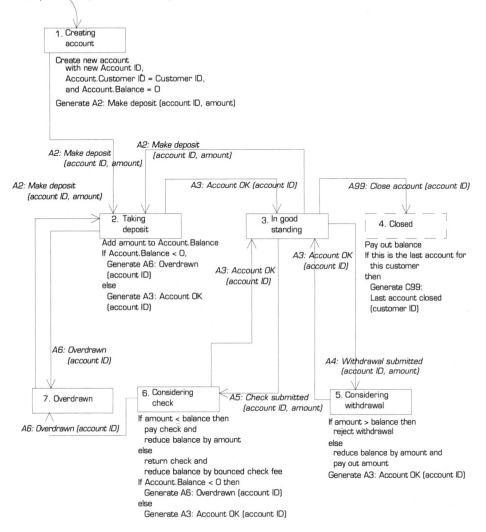

Figure 3.3.1: State model for the Account object

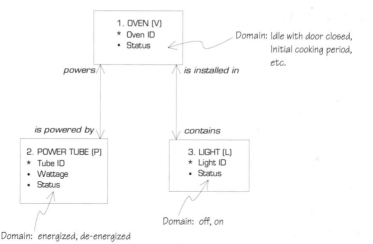

Figure 3.3.2: Information model for the one-minute microwave oven. Each object that has a state model must also have a current state or status attribute.

Final State

In some state models, one (or possibly several) states serve as the end of the lifecycle for an instance. Such states are known as *final states*. A final state may represent either of two situations:

> *The instance is becoming quiescent.* The instance continues to exist, but has no subsequent interesting dynamic behavior. No special notation is used on the STD for a final state in which the instance becomes quiescent.

> *The instance is ceasing to exist.* Once the instance comes into the state, the instance vanishes, and so therefore does its lifecycle. Such a state is indicated on the STD by a box drawn with dashed lines, as shown in Figure 3.3.1.

Current State

At any particular moment, different instances of an object may be in different states. The state an instance is in is known as its *current state*. The current state is represented by an attribute that is typically named "current state" or "status," as shown in Figure 3.3.2. This is a descriptive attribute; its domain is given by enumerating the states of the object's state model.

3.4 Events

An *event* is the abstraction of an incident or signal in the real world that tells us that something is moving to a new state. In abstracting an event, four aspects of the event are specified:

- meaning
- destination
- label
- event data

Meaning

The meaning of an event is captured in a short phrase that tells what is going on in the real world. In the case of the microwave oven, we have these meanings for the events: button pushed, cooking complete, door opened and door closed.

Destination

The destination of the event is the state model (not machine) that receives the event. There can be only one such receiver for a given event.

Label

A unique label must be provided for each event. The labels are required to distinguish different events from one another, particularly in the case when you have distinct events of similar meaning.

The form of an event label is arbitrary. We typically use a letter-number combination to produce short event labels such as the following for the microwave oven:

V1: Button pushed
V2: Cooking complete
V3: Door opened
V4: Door closed

Most analysts find it helpful to use some kind of a convention for assigning event labels. Here are two schemes that work reasonably well.

> ***Destination-based labeling.*** Define event labels so that all events that are received by an object begin with that object's key letter: P for the power tube, L for the light, and V for the oven.

Internal-external labeling. Use a particular letter (usually E for "external") to indicate an event that passes between two objects. For events that are generated by an object to itself, use the key letter assigned to that object.

Event Data

An event should be thought of as a control signal that can—and usually does—carry data. This data is supplied to the action on arrival in the state. Two different types of data can be carried by an event: identifier data and supplemental data.

Identifier data. Identifier data is a set of one or more attributes comprising the preferred identifier of the destination object. Identifier data specifies the instance—and therefore the state machine—that is going to receive the event.

Supplemental data. Supplemental data consists of one or more attributes carried by the event in addition to the identifier data. The supplemental data can supply attributes of any object, not just the destination object.

Event Data and States

There are a number of rules relating an event's data to the states that can be reached as a result of receiving the event.

Same data rule: All events that cause a transition into a particular state must carry exactly the same event data.

This rule guarantees that the action will receive the same event data regardless of which event causes the transition.

Non-creation state rule: If an event can cause a transition into a state that is not a creation state, the event must carry, as data, an identifier of the instance to which the event applies.

This rule guarantees that the action will be able to determine which existing instance has made the transition.

Creation state rule: An event that causes a transition into a creation state does not carry an identifier if the receiving state model creates the identifier in the action of the creation state.

Abstracting Events from Incidents

A single incident in the real world can be abstracted into more than one event. For example, suppose you have a railroad in which the trackage is divided into distinct track segments and that a train's position is defined as the track segment occupied by the leading car. Then the real-world incident of a train crossing into another segment might reasonably generate two events: one to the train to tell it that a new segment has been reached and one to the track segment that has just become occupied.

Event Specification vs. Event Instances

When an event (V1: button pushed, for example) appears on an STD, it represents the concept of a typical but unspecified occurrence of an incident—in this case, any button push on any microwave oven. This concept should be distinguished from the particular occurrences of V1: a button push on oven 5 at 3 p.m., another at 3:10, and a button push on oven 25 at 9 p.m. Both concepts are referred to informally as an event, and the meaning is generally clear from the context. However, when it is necessary to distinguish by means of terminology, we use *event specification* to refer to a typical unspecified occurrence (any button push on any oven) and *event instance* to refer to a particular occurrence (the button push on oven 5 at 3:10).

3.5 Actions

Actions and Instances

An *action* is an activity or operation that must be done by an instance upon arrival in a state. One action is associated with each state.

Because all instances of an object share the same state model, the actions must be defined in such a way that they can be executed by any instance.

When the action begins, it is provided with the event data carried by the event that caused the transition. The event data contains sufficient information to identify an existing instance on whose behalf the action is executing: In the case of a non-creation state, the event data includes an identifier of the instance.

In the case of a creation state, the action will create a new instance based on information carried in the event data. Once the instance has been created, the action can proceed to do additional work.

What an Action Can Do

An action typically reads and writes attributes of the instance for which it is executing. In addition, an action can:

1. Do any calculation.
2. Generate an event to any instance of any object (including the instance currently in execution).
3. Generate an event to something outside the scope of the analysis: an operator, a hardware device, or an object in another subsystem.
4. Create, delete, set, reset or read a timer (more about timers in Section 3.7).
5. Read and write attributes of other instances of its own object.
6. Read and write attributes of instances of other objects.

Note that allowing an action to read or write another object's attributes *in the analysis models* does not violate the design principle of encapsulation. One purpose of the analysis is to determine what data accesses are required between objects; the need to access another object's data is expressed in the analysis models as a read or write of that data.

What an Action *Must* Do

To ensure consistency of the state models as a whole, certain responsibilities must be assigned to the actions.

Leave the instance consistent. An action must leave data describing its own instance consistent. If an action updates an attribute of its own instance, it must update all attributes that are computationally dependent on the first attribute. For example, suppose we have two objects

Gas in Gas Bottle (<u>Gas Name</u>, <u>Bottle ID</u> (R), Temperature, Pressure)
Gas Bottle (<u>Bottle ID</u>, Volume)

Then if an action of Gas in Gas Bottle updates the temperature attribute, it must also update the pressure attribute.

Ensure consistency of relationships. If an action creates or deletes instances of its own object, it must ensure that any relationships involving those instances are made consistent with the rules stated on the information model. For example, consider these two objects:

Customer (<u>Customer ID</u>, Address)
Account (<u>Account Number</u>, Balance, Customer ID (R))

There is a one-to-many relationship between a customer and his account(s). Therefore, if an action of Account deletes the last account held by a particular customer, it must either (1) delete that customer directly or (2) generate an event to that customer instance which tells the customer that he is an ex-customer—that is, the event must tell the customer to delete himself.

Leave subtypes and supertypes consistent. The action must leave subtypes and supertypes consistently populated. Therefore, if an action creates an instance of the supertype object, it must also create an instance of exactly one of the subtype objects. Similarly, if an action deletes an instance of a subtype, it must also delete the corresponding instance of the supertype.

Update current state attribute. An action must update the current state attribute to correspond with the state the instance is now occupying as a result of executing the action. But note that since all actions must do this, some analysts and projects omit this step from the STD by convention.

Action Description

A description must be provided for each action. If the descriptions are not too lengthy, they are placed on the STD just below the appropriate state box; otherwise, they can be provided in a separate document.

Actions are described in a pseudocode of the analyst's choice. We have not prescribed a complete syntax for the pseudocode, but have found it helpful to establish the following conventions:

1. To generate an event, write

     Generate <event label>: <event meaning> (<event data>)

   as in

     Generate P1: Energize power tube (Tube ID)

2. Refer to an attribute as <object name>.<attribute name>. For example,

     Account.Customer ID

3. Refer to an attribute value of a particular instance as <object name>.<attribute name> (identifier)

     Account.Balance (account ID)

4. Indicate a particular value for an attribute by enclosing the value in quotation marks. For example,

Oven.Status (oven ID) := "cooking interrupted"

Actions, Events, and Time

The formalism makes certain assumptions about time with respect to actions, events, and state machines.

1. Only one action of a given state machine can be in execution at any point in time. Once initiated, the action must complete before another event can be received by this instance's state machine.

2. Actions in different state machines can be executing simultaneously.

3. Events are never lost.

4. If an event is generated to an instance that is currently executing an action, the event will not be accepted until after the action is complete.

5. Every event is used up when it is submitted to a state machine: The event then vanishes as an event.

Remembering Events

As a consequence of the "event used up when received" assumption, we can have a situation in which a state model receives an event that will affect the future behavior of the object, but that cannot be responded to while the instance is in the current state. In this situation the event must be remembered —either in data or in states. The following example illustrates two strategies for remembering events.

Figure 3.5.1 shows a portion of a plant that produces hair and skin care products such as shampoos and lotions. The mixing tank is first filled with the product's ingredients. The mixer is then turned on for a certain time period, after which the product is ready to be transferred to a bottling tank.

The product transfer can take place only after two conditions are established: (1) the mixing time is complete and (2) the bottling tank has been selected and its input valve opened. Since these conditions are achieved in separate incidents, they must be abstracted as two separate events:

M3: Mixing complete (mixing tank ID)
M4: Bottling tank ready for product (mixing tank ID)

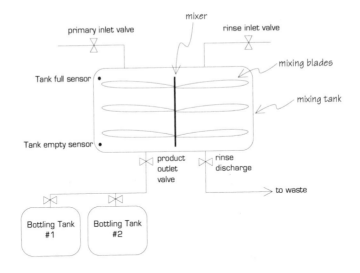

Figure 3.5.1: A portion of the cosmetics plant.

That is, you *cannot* abstract an event

    M100: Mixing complete and bottling tank ready

to represent the compound condition.

Since each part of the compound condition can be achieved independently, the mixing tank's lifecycle must accommodate the arrival of the events M3 and M4 in either order, as shown in Figure 3.5.2. In this solution, the early arrival of event M4 is remembered by causing the mixing tank to occupy the Mixing While Ready to Empty state.

An alternative solution requires an additional object

    Product Transfer (<u>Source Tank ID</u>, Destination Tank ID)

When the bottling tank becomes ready for the product, it creates an instance of Product Transfer *in addition to* generating event M4. The mixing tank's lifecycle is altered as shown in Figure 3.5.3.

If event M4 arrives when the mixing tank is in the Mixing Product state, the event is ignored, but is later regenerated by the mixing tank from the data trace of the earlier event left in Product Transfer. When using such a strategy, remember that the mixing tank must delete the instance of Product Transfer so that it does not try to reuse the trace on the next round through its lifecycle.

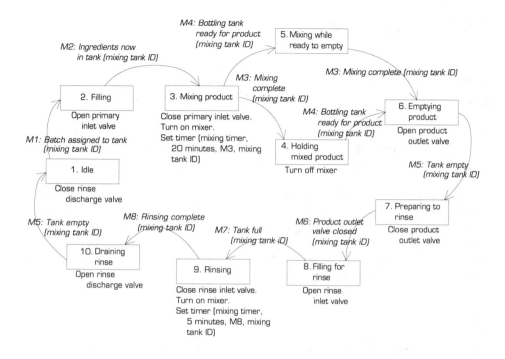

Figure 3.5.2: State model for the mixing tank. States 4 and 5 allow for the arrival of events M3 and M4 in any order.

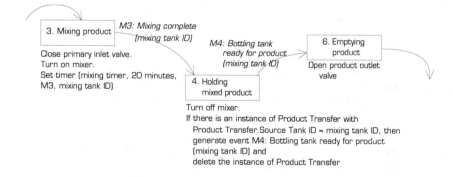

Figure 3.5.3: Modification for the mixing tank state model. If event M4 arrives before M3 it is ignored, but a record of it remains in an instance of Product Transfer.

3.6 Transitions and the State Transition Table

Transition Rules

Every state model has a set of transition rules (or transitions, for short) that specify what happens—what new state is achieved—if a particular event occurs while in a certain state. A transition is represented on the STD by an arrow from one state to another. The arrow is labeled with the event (label and meaning) that causes an instance to progress from one state to its successor.

Alternatively, the transition rules can be presented in a state transition table, as shown in Figure 3.6.1. In a state transition table (STT), each row represents one of the possible states of the state model, and each column represents an event that has this state model as its destination. The cells of the table are filled in to specify what happens when an instance in a given state (the row) receives a particular event (the column).

Cell Entries

The cells in the STT are filled with entries of three different types:

1. new state
2. event ignored
3. can't happen

New state entry. The cell is filled in with the name of the new state that results when an instance in the state specified by the row receives the event specified by the column. A new state entry corresponds exactly to a transition arrow on the STD.

Note that an event can cause an instance to transition into the state it is already in. In this case, the "new state" entry is, of course, the same as the state specified by the row. Nonetheless, this is considered to be a real transition, and it causes the instance to re-execute the action.

Event ignored. If an object refuses to respond to a particular event when it is in a certain state, enter "event ignored" in the appropriate cell. When an event is ignored, the instance stays in the same state it is in and *does not* re-execute the action. In this way, event ignored is different from a transition to the same state.

Note that although the event is ignored in the sense of not causing a transition, the event is used up by the state model.

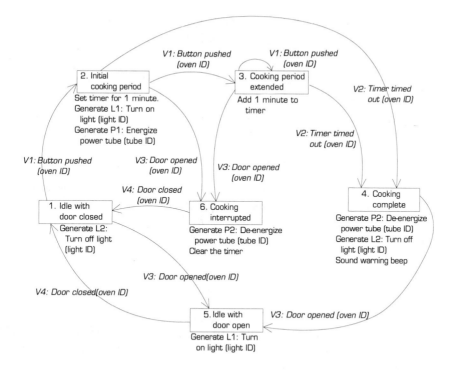

	V1: Button pushed	V2: Timer timed out	V3: Door opened	V4: Door closed
1. Idle with door closed	2	can't happen [1]	5	can't happen [3]
2. Initial cooking period	3	4	6	can't happen [3]
3. Cooking period extended	3	4	6	can't happen [3]
4. Cooking complete	event ignored	can't happen [1]	5	can't happen [3]
5. Idle with door open	event ignored	can't happen [1]	can't happen [2]	1
6. Cooking interrupted	event ignored	can't happen [1]	can't happen [2]	1

Notes:
[1] Timer is not running
[2] Door is already open
[3] Door is already closed

Figure 3.6.1: Lifecycle of the oven. The lifecycle can be represented by a state transition diagram or a state transition table.

Can't happen. If the event cannot happen when the instance is in a particular state, record that fact by entering "can't happen" in the appropriate cell. The "can't happen" entry is reserved for occasions when the event simply cannot occur in the real world. For example, the event V3: Door opened cannot happen when an oven is in state 5, since in that state the door is already open. Unless it is perfectly obvious, you should also explain why it is not possible for the event to occur. Such a note can appear as a footnote on the STT.

Role of the State Transition Table

Although the STT and the STD contain much of the same information, in practice we find that both forms are needed. The diagrammatic form of the STD is essential for understanding the lifecycle of the object; in our experience it is very difficult to understand (or develop) a lifecycle model working only with an STT.

On the other hand, the STT is a far superior representation for verifying the completeness and consistency of the transition rules. Filling out the STT requires you to consider the effect of every event-state combination. In addition, the tabular form prevents one from making inconsistent statements such as:

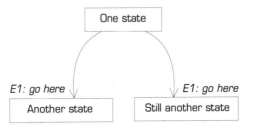

3.7 Timers

Concept of a Timer

A *timer* is a mechanism that can be used by an action to generate an event at some time in the future. The mechanism is part of the OOA formalism, and is

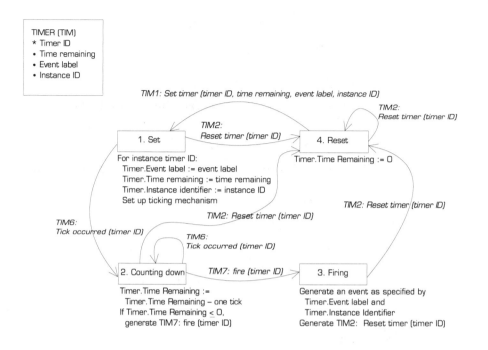

Figure 3.7.1: The Timer object together with its lifecycle.

supplied in the form of a Timer object (Figure 3.7.1). The attributes of Timer are:

- Timer ID: An identifier for the timer itself
- Time Remaining: The amount of time that must pass before the timer fires
- Event Label: The label of an event to be generated when the timer fires
- Instance ID: An identifier to be passed with the generated event

All timers operate according to the Timer state model (Figure 3.7.1), which assumes a simple countdown mechanism.

Pseudocode Conventions for Timers

The following conventions may be used in describing an action that makes use of timers.

1. To create a timer, write

   timer ID := Create timer

2. To set a timer, generate the event

   TIM1: Set timer (timer ID, time remaining, event label, instance ID)

   For example, for the microwave oven

   Generate TIM1: Set timer (oven timer, 60 seconds, V2, oven ID)

3. To reset a timer, generate the event

   TIM2: Reset timer (timer ID)

4. To read the time interval remaining on the timer, write

   still to go := Read time remaining (timer ID)

5. To delete a timer write

   Delete timer (timer ID)

Use of a Timer

Timers are commonly used to signify the expiration of a time interval required by an instrument or industrial process, as illustrated by the microwave oven. In addition, a timer can be used to drive an iterative or continuous operation; this use is demonstrated in Section 5.7. Finally, a timer can be used to protect against the failure of an event to arrive, as shown in Section 3.12.

3.8 Common Lifecycle Forms

While the state model for an object can have almost any shape, a few common patterns can be identified. We have found it useful to have terms to refer to these patterns.

Circular Lifecycle. Circular lifecycles generally arise when the object has an operational cycle of behavior. The microwave oven has such a circular nature, as does the drill robot (Figure 3.8.1).

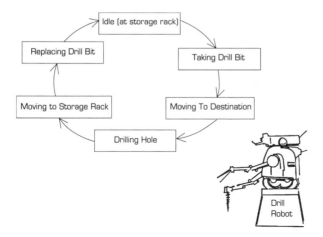

Figure 3.8.1: The drill robot's lifecycle. The actions have been omitted from the STD.

Born-and-Die Lifecycle. An object has a born-and-die lifecycle when instances are created and deleted within the lifetime of the system being analyzed. A born-and-die lifecycle is characterized by one or more creation states and one or more final states in which the instance is destroyed. The Account object examined earlier provides an example of a born-and-die lifecycle.

In a minor variant of this pattern, the instance is not deleted, and only becomes dormant in the final state.

3.9 Forming Lifecycles

Many people have learned to use state models to record the externally observable behavior of a device or system. This use of state models asks you to regard the device as a "black box" whose inner workings are unknown. States are formed in accordance with what can be observed from the outside, and actions are omitted since they are not visible from the outside.

By contrast, the state models of OOA seek to explain the details of the behavior from inside the device. Their purpose is an analysis purpose: to explicate details of behavior so that you can understand why an instance needs to behave in a certain way and what actions are required to make it behave properly. This use of state models is sometimes called a "white-box" or "clear-box" use.

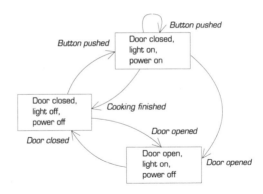

Figure 3.9.1: Black-box state transition diagram for the oven.

Very different models are produced depending on whether one takes a clear-box or a black-box perspective. This is illustrated by comparing the clear-box state model of the microwave oven (Figure 3.2.2) to a black-box view (Figure 3.9.1).

Since we have observed that it is easy to fall into a black-box mind-set when first building state models, here are some suggestions and guidelines that may help you to avoid this trap.

Purpose. In identifying states, it is important to remember that every state has a purpose. In Figure 3.5.2, the mixing tank is configured in exactly the same way in the Mixing Product and Rinsing states: the mixer is on and all valves are closed. Nonetheless, the purposes of the states are different, and are reflected in the names we choose for the states.

Context. Every state has a context. The meaning of a particular state may be established by the states that precede and follow it. Returning to the example of Figure 3.1.1, observe that if you spot an airplane moving along a taxiway you don't know why it is taxiing. But the states that precede and follow provide a context that tells you why: the plane is getting ready to take off or it is trying to get to the gate.

Full snapshots. Do not try to form states that reflect limited snapshots of reality. The Mixing Product and Rinsing states of the mixing tank look alike when you consider only what you might observe through sensor data: they require the same configuration of the valves and the state of the mixer. However, if you expand your view to take into account what is in the tank, the states become distinct.

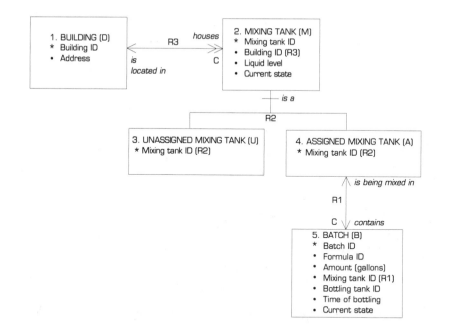

Figure 3.10.1: Information model for a portion of the cosmetics plant.

Actions. Pay attention to the actions. The Cooking Complete and Idle With Door Closed states of the microwave oven are distinct because their actions have to differ to make the oven work according to requirements.

3.10 Lifecycles for Subtypes and Supertypes

In a subtype-supertype construction, a single instance is represented in both the supertype and in the subtype object on the information model. This fact imposes certain additional rules for forming the lifecycles of subtype and supertype objects. There are several different cases to consider, each of which is described below.

Subtype Migration

When an instance of the supertype object migrates between the subtype objects, the lifecycle can be drawn at either the subtype or supertype level. Here is an example based on the cosmetics plant considered in Section 3.5. The pertinent part of the information model appears in Figure 3.10.1.

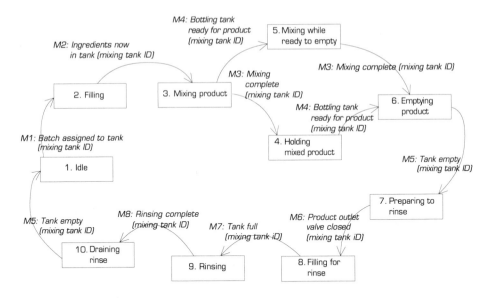

Figure 3.10.2: Lifecycle of the supertype object Mixing Tank.

Supertype lifecycle, migratory case. Figure 3.10.2 shows a lifecycle drawn at the supertype level. All events that drive this lifecycle have the Mixing Tank state model as their destination.

Subtype lifecycles, migratory case. The circular supertype lifecycle can be broken into two born-and-die cycles, one for each subtype. This is done by assigning a consecutive series of states to each subtype. The resulting subtype lifecycles are shown in Figure 3.10.3. Note that the events must now be directed to the subtype lifecycles.

Non-migrating Subtypes

When an instance of the supertype remains an instance of a single subtype throughout its entire existence, we have the non-migratory case. The lifecycles should then be formed according to the following discussion.

Supertype lifecycles, non-migratory case. If the dynamic behavior of an instance of the supertype does not depend on which subtype it belongs to, the lifecycle is formed at the supertype level, and events that drive the lifecycle are directed to the supertype. Note that you will almost certainly have some if-logic in the actions of such a lifecycle. This logic will be required if the subtypes have

Assigned Mixing Tank

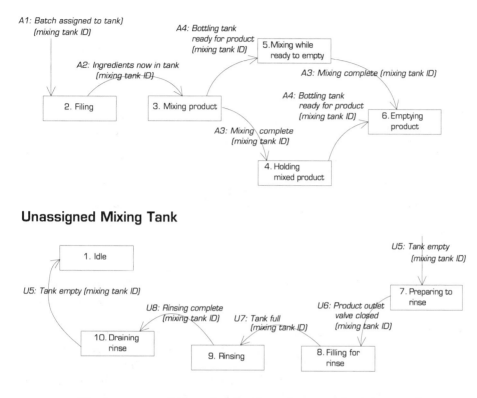

Figure 3.10.3: Lifecycles for the subtypes of Mixing Tank.

attributes of their own that attain values during the lifecycle, or if the subtypes enter into different relationships that must be maintained by the actions.

Subtype lifecycles, non-migratory case. If the dynamic behavior of an instance depends entirely on which subtype it belongs to, lifecycles are formed separately for each subtype. Events that drive the lifecycles must be directed to each separate subtype, as appropriate.

Splicing. Finally, it is possible that most of the dynamic behavior of an instance does not depend on which subtype it belongs to, but that for a part of the lifecycle, the behavior differs according to which subtype is involved. This idea is shown in Figure 3.10.4. All instances behave the same way as they progress from state II to state I. They then behave differently, each according to its subtype, until they reach state II.

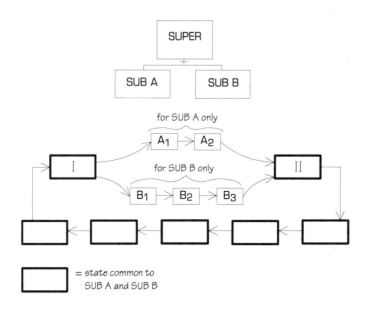

Figure 3.10.4: Spliced state models for subtype-supertype objects.

This kind of behavior could be documented properly by producing a separate and complete state model for each subtype. However, this will present a maintenance problem, in that the same information—the shared portion of the lifecycle—must be accurately maintained in every subtype's state model. As an alternative, then, the analyst can produce the common portion of the lifecycle as a state model for the supertype and the individual portions of the lifecycle as state models for each subtype. In so doing, observe the following:

- Events that cause transitions into or within the common portion of the lifecycle are directed at the supertype object.

- Events that cause transitions into or within the subtype portions of the lifecycle are directed at the subtypes.

3.11 When to Form Lifecycles

Although, in principle, all objects have lifecycles, it is necessary to build state models to formalize the lifecycles for only some of the objects. The following suggestions should help you decide which objects need this treatment. Please note that these are only guidelines: as always with these knowledge-formalization tasks, you must still use your own judgment in the particular situation you are facing.

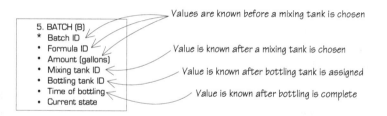

Figure 3.11.1: Instances of this object gather values for their attributes as they progress through their lifecycles.

The master guideline is this: If the object has interesting, pertinent, dynamic behavior, formalize the lifecycle; otherwise don't bother. Now for some details and examples.

Run time creation or destruction. If instances of an object are created or destroyed (or archived, retired, deleted, and so on) in run time, the lifecycle should be formalized. The Account is an example of such an object.

Migration between subtypes. If instances of the object migrate from one subtype to another, the lifecycle should be formalized.

Accumulation of attributes. If instances gather values for their attributes as they progress through their lifecycles, the lifecycle should be formalized. See Figure 3.11.1 for an example of such an object.

Operational cycle of equipment. An equipment-based object that exhibits a distinct operational cycle should have its lifecycle formalized. The drill robot and the mixing tank provide examples of such an object.

Object is manufactured or comes into being in stages. An object that comes into existence step by step should have its lifecycle formalized.

Task or request. An object that represents a request or a task to be done should probably have its lifecycle formalized.

Dynamic relationships. If the instances of the object move in and out of relationships, the lifecycle should be formalized.

Linked lifecycles. If an object represents equipment whose normal operation or malfunction causes another object to progress through its lifecycle, the lifecycles of both objects need to be formalized.

Passive facility. If an object represents a facility that is entirely passive, its lifecycle probably does not need to be formalized. For example, the Building object in Figure 3.10.1 is entirely passive (although it contains equipment that has significant dynamic behavior).

Specification objects. If an object represents a specification, quality standard, or recipe, its lifecycle probably does not need to be formalized.

3.12 Failure Analysis

Abnormal Behavior

In the examples considered so far, we have studied only the normal or desired behavior of various objects. In this section we take up the subject of abnormal behavior, a catch-all term that includes notions of errors, failures, and unusual and/or undesirable behavior. The investigation of abnormal behavior is frequently termed failure analysis. The treatment given here is not intended to be comprehensive; failure analysis is a wide-ranging subject and is highly problem dependent. In this section we focus on examples pertinent to real-time systems.

The purpose of failure analysis is to study the effect of certain kinds of malfunctions and errors and to evaluate strategies for dealing with them. The higher goal is usually to maintain or recover control of an industrial or other external process. As a result, failure analysis frequently leads to statements of previously unanticipated requirements, installation of additional sensors, formalization of operating procedures in the plant, and the like.

Failure Analysis in OOA

In OOA, abnormal behavior is formalized in state models in exactly the same way as is normal behavior. A recommended procedure is this: First, model the normal, desirable behavior of the objects in state models as we have done throughout this chapter. Second, add states, events, and actions to the "normal behavior" models to capture abnormal behavior that arises in the external process or plant. Finally, extend the resulting state models to account for sensor and actuator failures.

The key issue in extending the state models to cover abnormal behavior is, of course, identifying sources of errors and failures. We have found two approaches useful: one based on examining the external process, and one based on a systematic walkthrough of the OOA models. These are described in subsequent sections.

Failures in the External Process and Interface Equipment

Here are some broad questions to consider in looking for sources of failure in the external process.

Equipment failure or malfunction. These failures include things like loss of power, stuck valves, tripped breakers, overtemperature conditions, and the like. Many conditions of this sort will be sensed; they are, as a result, fairly well known and easy to identify. Less easy are unsensed conditions such as leaks.

Personnel error. Personnel errors include such things as routing a train onto the wrong track or opening a valve at the wrong time (either through a computer or via manual control).

Problems related to time. The mixing problem considered earlier provides an excellent example: Suppose the mixed product is retained in the mixing tank for a long time while the bottling tank is readied. Is it possible that the ingredients could begin to settle out and another mixing cycle be required?

Sensor failures. A sensor can fail in such a way that it indicates that a circuit breaker, for example, is tripped when in fact it is not. Sensor failures can sometimes be distinguished from true equipment problems by inspecting additional sensed data. In the case of the mixing tank, we may be able to determine whether the product exhaust valve is really open or closed by checking the level sensors in both the mixing tank and the bottling tank.

Actuator failure. An actuator failure occurs when the computer commands an external device to do something, but the external device does not respond. Some actuator failures can be detected by the use of a timer and a corresponding sensed value: Generate a command to an external device and set a timer for a time interval in which the device should respond. If the device responds before the timer expires, as evidenced by an appropriate change in a sensed value, the actuator worked properly and the timer should be reset. If, however, the timer expires before the device responds, the actuator may have failed.

Identifying Failures through the OOA Models

We can frequently identify sources of failure by examining the "normal behavior" OOA state models in a systematic fashion. Here are some questions and guidelines for identifying potential sources of failures:

1. For each state, what incident in the real world could force the instance to a new state? For example, if the rinse inlet valve were to open when the Mixing Tank is in the Mixing state, the product in the mixing tank would be contaminated with rinse solution. Hence you would need to make a new state to handle this situation.

2. Is each event guaranteed to occur? This question will pick up certain sensor and actuator errors, as well as some operational errors.

3. If an event occurs, does it mean what it normally does?

4. Is each event guaranteed to occur in a timely fashion? What happens to the process if the event is delayed?

5. Is each action guaranteed to have the expected effect under all circumstances?

Final Note

Before leaving the subject of failure analysis, we would like to sound a cautionary note. Once the subject of abnormal behavior comes up, it is easy to get carried away and investigate myriads of possible failures, from the real and reasonable to the outstandingly far-fetched. Abnormal behavior can be very complex, and the models become correspondingly larger and more complicated as more and more abnormal cases are considered. This is the time to draw upon the best engineering judgment available in your particular situation, and use it to prioritize the cases investigated and to keep the work within bounds.

3.13 Work Products

State Models

Each object that has a state model is documented by providing:

- A state transition diagram (STD)
- A state transition table (STT)
- A description of each action on the state transition diagram (required only if the actions were too long to put on the STD)

Event List

Label	Meaning	Event Date	Source	Destination
V1	Button pushed	oven ID	button	oven
V2	Timer timed out	oven ID	oven timer	oven
L1	Turn on light	light ID	oven	light
P1	Energize power tube	tube ID	oven	power tube
...	...	...	...	...

Figure 3.13.1: Recommended form for the Event List.

Event List

An event list is simply a listing of all the events that have been defined for all the state models. The recommended form for an event list is shown in Figure 3.13.1.

We have found that a spreadsheet, database or CASE tool is extremely useful for maintaining the event list. Such a tool makes it easy to sort the events in various orders that are useful for understanding and checking the state models. In particular, consider sorting the event list

- alphabetically by event labels.
- by the source state model.
- by the destination state model.

References

[1] E. F. Moore, "Gedanken-experiments on Sequential Machines." In *Automata Studies*, Princeton University Press, Princeton N. J., 1956.

4 Dynamics of Relationships

This chapter explains how to formalize the dynamic behavior of relationships and how to deal with contention in the analysis.

4.1 Relationship Dynamics

Associations between some things in the real world evolve over time, with different rules and policies pertaining at different points in the duration of the association.

When we formalize a real-world association as a relationship on the information model, we capture only the static aspect of the association: must it or can it exist? What we do not capture is the dynamics of the relationship:

> How does the relationship evolve over time?
> Under what circumstances is an instance of a relationship created or destroyed?
> How are instances of objects selected to participate in a relationship?

Questions such as these are answered in state models—either in the state models of the participating objects or in separate state models for the relationships themselves. In this chapter we consider the various components of the dynamic behavior of a relationship and show how this behavior is captured in state models.

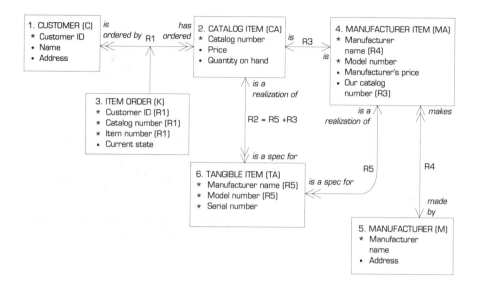

Figure 4.2.1: Information model for distributor's operation.

4.2 Lifecycles of Relationships

In some cases, an association between real-world things progresses through distinct stages during which different rules and policies apply. When this is the case, the association is abstracted as a relationship in the form of an associative object with a current state attribute. A state model is then built to formalize the lifecycle of the relationship.

The state model prescribes the behavior of a typical unspecified instance of the relationship. All instances of the relationship execute this same state model; as with an object, we use the term state machine to refer to the execution of the state model by a particular instance of the relationship.

Example. A distributor offers various types of electronic equipment for sale. The sales department processes incoming customer purchase orders, breaking each purchase order into separate "item orders," each of which represents a request for a single piece of equipment. In the information model (Figure 4.2.1), the relationship Customer HAS ORDERED Catalog Item is captured in the associative object Item Order.

Item Order

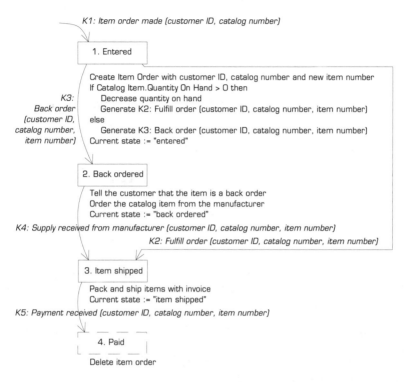

Figure 4.2.2: State model for the Item Order object.

Within the distributor's operation, each item order is processed separately: the equipment needed to satisfy the item order is obtained from stock and then packed, shipped, and invoiced. This strategy has come about because some items are easily available and can be shipped almost immediately, while others may require a wait of some weeks while new stock is obtained from the manufacturer.

The lifecycle of the item order appears in Figure 4.2.2. Note that although Item Order came about because of a relationship, its state model is built in exactly the same way as is the state model for an object.

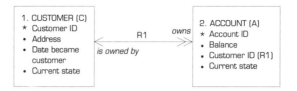

Figure 4.3.1: Excerpt from the information model of a bank.

4.3 Dynamic Relationships without Lifecycles

If a relationship does not have a lifecycle, it may still have dynamic behavior if instances of the relationship are created or deleted during the time scope of the analysis. For example, in a banking application the relationship between a customer and his account is permanent and has no stages in which different rules apply. However, whenever a customer or an account is created or deleted, an instance of the Customer OWNS Account relationship must be correspondingly created or deleted.

> A customer is any person or organization who has established at least one account.
> New customers can be added at any time.
> New accounts can be created at any time.
> If a customer closes his last account, he is no longer a customer.

The information model appears in Figure 4.3.1.

Since the only dynamic behavior of the relationship is concerned with the creation and deletion of instances of the relationship, a state model does not need to be built for the relationship. Instead, the relationship instances are created and deleted by the state models of the participating objects, as shown in Figure 4.3.2.

4.4 Relationships Involving Competition: The Monitor

Competition in the Real World

In the real world there may or may not be competition associated with establishing a relationship. In the Customer–Item Order example, customers do not have to compete with one another to make an Item Order; the distributor

Customer

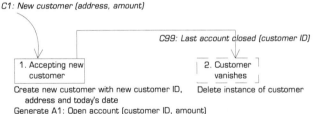

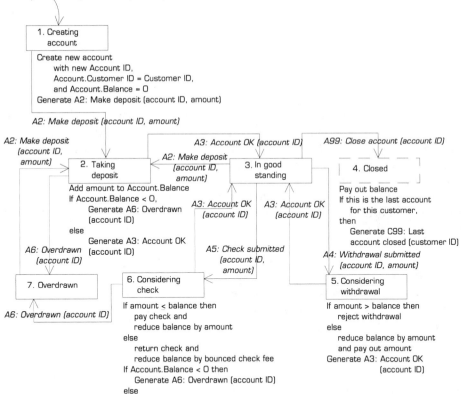

Figure 4.3.2: State models for Customer and Account.

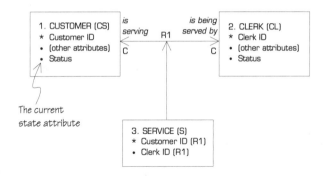

Figure 4.4.1: Information model for Customer-Clerk problem.

can accept as many orders as he wants. Similarly, in the banking example, there is an unending supply of new accounts, and any customer's request to open a new account can be honored.

By contrast, consider a situation in which customers (patients, passengers, and the like) compete for the attention of a limited number of clerks (physicians, waiters, or flight attendants). When a clerk becomes available, the unserved customers attempt to capture the attention of the clerk in order to form an instance of the one-to-one relationship Customer IS BEING SERVED BY Clerk. Since the customers—now viewed as OOA instances—operate concurrently, it is possible for two customers to bid for the clerk's attention at precisely the same time. In the absence of any control mechanism, the clerk could be claimed by both customers simultaneously.

Contention problems such as this must be solved by providing a single control point through which competing requests are serialized. In the real world, this serialization can be enforced by a variety of mechanisms: a line of customers (a manifestation of a policy requiring that customers be served in order of their arrival) or a person who assigns customers to clerks based on some other policy (for example, in a hospital emergency room, the severity of the "customer's" condition is likely to be the dominant consideration). In OOA, the serialization is accomplished by a special state model for the relationship in which there is competition.

Competition in OOA

When dealing with a relationship in which there is competition, we must first formalize the relationship as an associative object on the information model (as

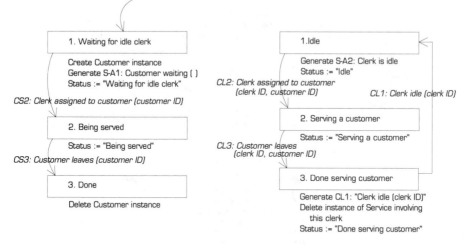

Figure 4.4.2: State models for Customer and Clerk.

in Figure 4.4.1). Next we build a state model that is responsible for creating instances of the relationship by associating instances of the participating objects with one another. This state model is named for the associative object of the relationship:

> <name of associative object> Assigner.

Events directed to this state model are labeled

> <key letter of the associative object>–A

Because the purpose of the Assigner is to act as the single point of control through which competing requests are serialized, there is only one copy of this state model. The current state of the Assigner is kept in the state model itself and does not appear as an attribute on the information model.

Monitors

The Assigner state model can take various different forms, depending on the semantics of the situation. In this section, we present a fundamental form known as a monitor.

Service Assigner

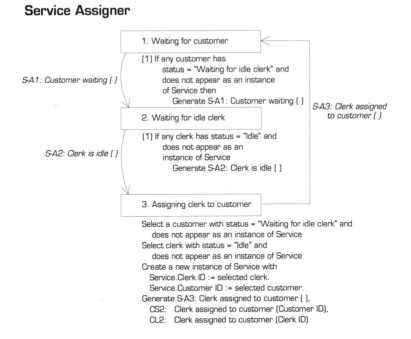

Figure 4.4.3: State model for Service Assigner.

The state models for Customer, Clerk, and Service Assigner (the monitor) are shown in Figures 4.4.2 and 4.4.3. To understand the operation of the monitor, first assume that the monitor is in state 1 (Waiting for Customer) and that the action has already been executed. When a customer requests a clerk (state 1 of Customer), the event S-A1: Customer Waiting () is generated. The monitor receives this event and makes the transition to state 2.

Arriving in state 2, the monitor executes the action. The monitor determines if there is a free clerk by examining the Status attribute of all clerks (ignoring for the moment the "and" clause of the action). If any clerk is idle, the monitor generates the event S-A2: Clerk Idle (). If no clerk is idle, the monitor remains in state 2 until an instance of clerk generates S-A2: Clerk Idle ().

The event S-A2: Clerk Idle () takes the monitor to state 3. Note that the monitor can only arrive in state 3 when a clerk is idle and a customer is waiting. The action selects an idle clerk and a waiting customer according to an appropriate policy. Events are then generated to each of the assigned instances. In addition, an event is generated to the monitor to cause it to go to state 1 to see if any more customers are now waiting.

	S-A1 Customer Waiting	S-A2 Clerk is Idle	S-A3 Clerk Assigned to Customer
1. Waiting for Customer	2	event ignored	can't happen
2. Waiting for Idle Clerk	event ignored	3	can't happen
3. Assigning Clerk to Customer	event ignored	event ignored	1

Figure 4.4.4: State transition table for the Service Assigner.

Note that the monitor ignores (that is, discards) Customer Waiting events while in states 2 and 3, and Clerk Idle events while in states 3 and 1. However, the fact that a customer has arrived or a clerk has become idle is retained in the current state attribute of each instance. The monitor depends fundamentally on the values of these attributes to move from state to state.

Now for the "and" clauses: Because the order in which events are processed is not defined*, it could happen that the monitor assigns customer X to a clerk while in monitor state 3 and that customer X has not yet processed its Clerk Assigned event at the time the monitor arrives in state 1. The customer will therefore still have a current state of Waiting for Idle Clerk. Obviously, the monitor does not want to pick customer X again, so it checks the Service instances to verify that the customer has not already been picked.

Note that events generated to the monitor do not carry identifier data. Since there is only one copy of the monitor state machine, there is no need to identify the instance.

Instance Selection

In the Customer–Clerk example, the state machine managing the relationship made the selection between customers and clerks arbitrarily. In the typical case, however, a more complex selection policy will be required. This frequently requires that additional attributes be assigned to the objects participating in the relationship (or to other nearby objects) in order to support the policy desired. For example, should you wish to assign customers preferentially to the clerks who have served the fewest customers to date, an attribute Clerk.Number of Customers Served would have to be added to Clerk. Alterna-

---

*This is discussed in some detail in Chapter 5.

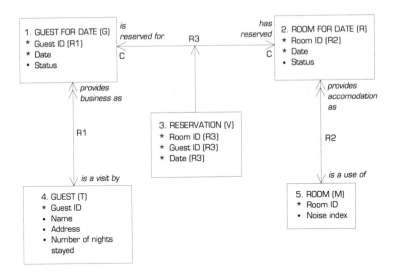

Figure 4.5.1: Information model for hotel room problem.

tively, the selection policy could take into account the time of arrival of the customer (Customer.Time of Arrival), the age of the customer, or how long he has been doing business with the organization that is providing the service.

4.5 The General Case of a Competitive Relationship

Building a state model to create the instances of a competitive relationship generally takes some careful thought; the simple monitor form is directly applicable only in certain situations. This section presents a systematic procedure for building the required Assigner state model in the general case. The procedure is illustrated through an example involving a hotel with a finite number of rooms. Guests compete with one another to reserve rooms for various dates.

Step 1: Information Model

As always, we build the information model first. The competitive relationship must be formalized as an associative object. Any attributes required to support the intended selection policy should be supplied for the appropriate objects. The information model for the hotel room problem is shown in Figure 4.5.1.

Guest for Date   **Room for Date**

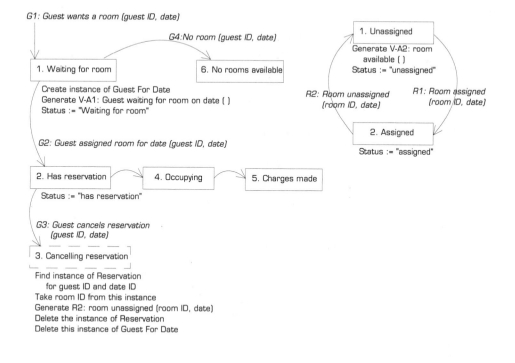

Figure 4.5.2: State models for hotel room problem.

The attributes of Guest and Room provide for a selection policy that gives the quietest rooms to the most frequent guests.

Step 2: State Models for Participating Objects

Build state models for both objects that participate in the relationship. Identify any events the object state models expect to receive from the Assigner state model.

Figure 4.5.2 shows the state models for Guest for Date and Room for Date. The events we plan to generate from the Assigner state model are

G2: Guest assigned room for date (guest ID, date)
G4: No room (guest ID, date)
R1: Room assigned (room ID, date)

Reservation Assigner (Incorrect)

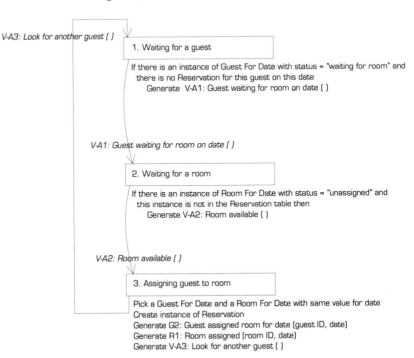

Figure 4.5.3: First draft of state model for Reservation Assigner.

Step 3: Assigner State Model, First Draft

Build the first draft of the Assigner state model in the form of a monitor. The purpose of this version of the state model is to work out the logic of the communicating events. Hence, details of the selection process that involve finding instances qualified to participate in the relationship must be included. However, those aspects of the selection process that choose *among* qualified instances (time of arrival of a customer, quietness of a room, and so on) should be omitted. The first-draft state model for the hotel problem is shown in Figure 4.5.3.

Step 4: Revise the First Draft

Examine the first-draft Assigner model to see if it fails and why. Verify that the events expected by the participating objects are generated.

Reservation Assigner (Correct)

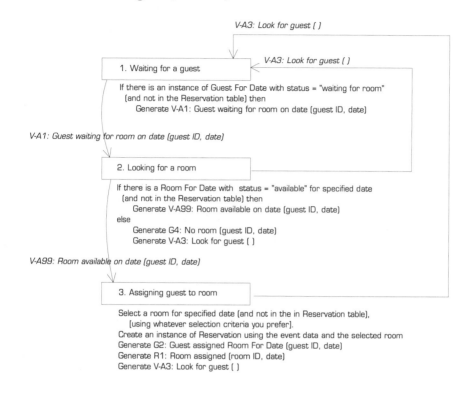

Figure 4.5.4: Final version of Reservation Assigner state model.

In the first-draft model of Figure 4.5.3, it is possible that you could get to state 3 and find that all guests were waiting for rooms for a date when the hotel was full and that there were rooms available for other dates. In this case, the action could not be executed.

This implies that state 2 should be inspecting rooms only for dates for which guests are waiting. On the revised state model of Figure 4.5.4,

- The event V-A1 has been redefined so that it carries the pertinent data—in this case, the date—as supplementary data.

- The action of state 2 considers only rooms for a specified date. If the action determines that a reservation can be made, an event is generated to carry us to state 3 in the normal way. If a reservation cannot be made,

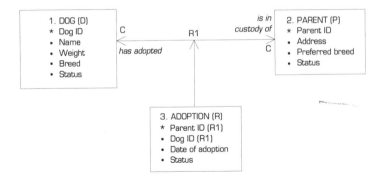

Figure 4.6.1: Information model for the dog adoption agency.

the action generates (1) the (previously missing) event G4 to tell the guest that the reservation cannot be made, and (2) another event to carry us to state 1 to select a more promising guest.

Note that we are now using a new event (V-A99) to get us to state 3. This is because the event previously used for this purpose (V-A2) may apply to a date for which we have no waiting guests. The rule is that when you reach the state that makes the assignment, the action must be able to execute successfully.

Step 5: Revise the State Models of Participating Objects

Minor adjustments are generally required to make the object state models consistent with the Assigner model. In particular, make sure that events generated by the participating objects carry all (and only) the data actually used by the Assigner model. It may also be that some events are no longer necessary. In the hotel example, Room for Date no longer needs to generate V-A2: Room available.

4.6 Competitive Relationships with Instance Lifecycles

Some relationships require an instance lifecycle state model as well as an Assigner state model. Consider the following situation: a high-class dog-adoption agency that accepts only purebred dogs for placement for adoption. Citizens so inclined can register at the adoption agency to receive a dog of a particular breed. The information model for the dog-adoption agency is shown in Figure 4.6.1.

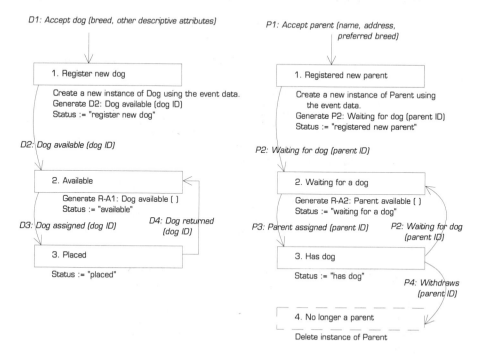

Figure 4.6.2: State models for Dog and Parent.

The agency matches the dogs available for adoption and the potential adoptive "parents." Once the match has been made, the parent pays an adoption fee. The state models for the Dog and adoptive Parent are shown in Figure 4.6.2. Of course, a state model is also required to serialize competing requests of parents for dogs; this model (Adoption Assigner) appears in Figure 4.6.3.

So far, this is very similar to the hotel room and guest problem—but now there is a new twist: Once a dog has been placed for adoption, the adoption is considered probationary for six months. At any time during that period, the parent can return the dog to the agency and receive a refund of the adoption fee. The parent can then be matched with another dog and the dog with another parent. Alternatively, the parent may choose to withdraw as an adoptive parent.

After six months, the adoption is considered to be final. If the adoptive parents return the dog to the agency after the adoption is final, the adoption fee is not

Adoption Assigner

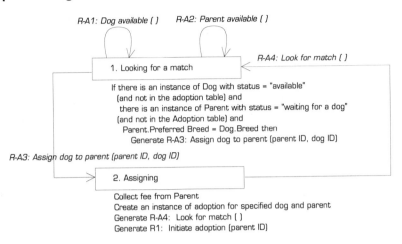

Figure 4.6.3: State model for Adoption Assigner.

refunded. However, the adoptive parents can be matched with another dog if they so request.

The individual instances of Adoption clearly have separate lifecycles. The state model for the instances of Adoption is shown in Figure 4.6.4.

Note that it is relatively uncommon to find a relationship that requires an Assigner as well as a state model to formalize the dynamics of the individual relationship instances. Nonetheless, it can happen, so the analyst is advised to be alert to this possibility.

4.7 Modeling Suggestions

Here are some specific suggestions you may find helpful when constructing the state models for both objects and relationships.

Get the information model right. Experience indicates that if you are having significant problems in constructing the state models, there is probably something wrong with the information model. The best strategy then is to turn to the information model and see what additional insight you have gained

Adoption (Instances)

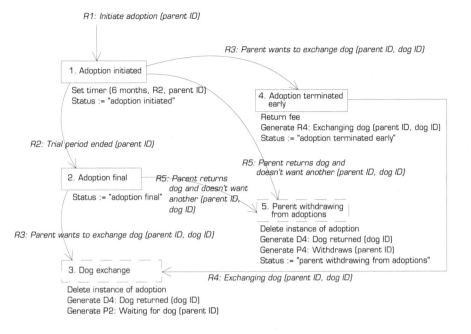

Figure 4.6.4: State model for Adoption Instances.

while struggling with the state models. A minor revision of the information model is frequently all that is needed to make the state models come together.

Keep the events under control. Nothing is more confusing than a set of models with inconsistent event labels, variant meanings, and uncertain event data. It is usually best to rely on the event list as the official definition of the events and to make the state models conform to the event list.

Watch out for the monitor trap. Competitive relationships can be fairly tricky, so it is easy to fall into the trap of writing down the monitor form for an Assigner state model without really thinking through the specific situation.

Use an object communication model. The object communication model (described in Chapter 5) is a graphic representation of event communication between different objects and relationships. If you sketch a rough object communication model early and maintain it as you proceed, you are less likely to become overwhelmed by the events.

5

System Dynamics

The state models for objects and relationships provide a detailed description of the dynamics of each separate component of the system. In this chapter, we turn our attention to understanding the dynamics of the system as a whole.

5.1 Object Communication Model

The object communication model, or OCM, provides a graphical summary of event communication between state models and external entities such as operators, physical devices, and objects in other subsystems. Each state model is represented on the OCM by a flattened oval labeled with the name of the state model. Each external entity that can generate or receive events is depicted by a box, known as a terminator. An event that is generated by one state model or external entity and received by another is represented by an arrow from the generating component to the receiver. The arrow is annotated with the event label, meaning, and (optionally) event data.

A sample OCM is shown in Figure 5.1.1. Note that, by convention, events generated or received by timers are omitted from the OCM, since experience indicates that such events contribute little to our understanding of the system as a whole. For the same reason, we omit events that are generated and received by the same state model.

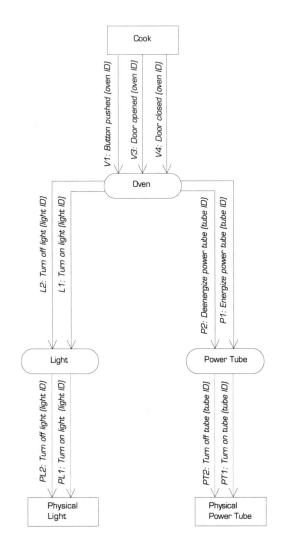

Figure 5.1.1: Object communication model for the
microwave oven.

While the OCM can be built directly from the state models, we find it somewhat
easier to work from the event list, extracting all entries where the event source
and destination are different.

5.2   Layering of Objects

Intelligence, Context, and Purpose

In the microwave oven example, you may have observed that the lifecycle of the oven was qualitatively different from those of the power tube and light. The purpose of the oven's lifecycle was to coordinate the operation of the power tube and light in order to make this ensemble of equipment act like a microwave oven: as a result, the oven's state model has qualities of intelligence, context, and purpose. By contrast, the state models of the power tube and light have an obedient character, compatible with their limited awareness of the system as a whole.

In a larger model, one sees this pattern successively, wherein objects with much purpose and intelligence delegate work to less intelligent objects and coordinate their lifecycles as the work is carried out. This is nicely demonstrated by the juice plant example [1]. A sketch of a portion of the juice plant is shown in Figure 5.2.1, and the corresponding information model is given in Figure 5.2.2. The object communication model is shown in Figure 5.2.3.

The Batch object represents a batch of juice from the time it is scheduled to be manufactured until it is put into cans for consumers.

Supporting the Batch are objects representing manufacturing steps: a Juice Transfer, a Temperature Ramp, and a Canning Operation. An instance of Batch causes itself to become manufactured by delegation:

> The Batch state model creates one or more Juice Transfers in order to cause juice to be piped into the Cooking Tank (event JT1: Do juice transfer).

> It then creates a Temperature Ramp so that the juice will be heated slowly to the pasteurization temperature (event TR90: Do temperature ramp).

> It creates another Temperature Ramp to cause the juice to be held at the pasteurization temperature for a prescribed time (event TR90: Do temperature ramp).

> Finally, it creates a Canning Operation to cause the batch of juice to be transferred to a canning line and packaged for delivery to the consumer.

The effect of this delegation is that Batch does not need to know the details of how the equipment is manipulated to accomplish the required manufacturing process.

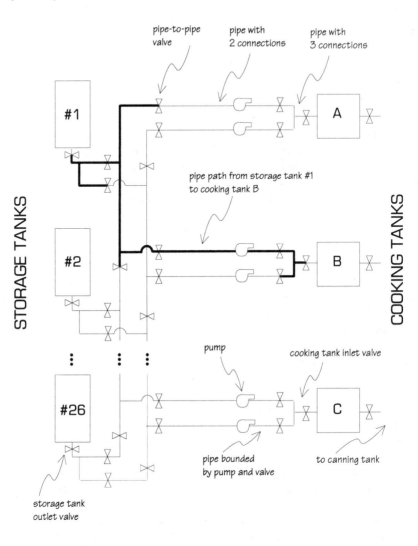

Figure 5.2.1: Layout of a portion of the juice plant.

Similarly, the Juice Transfer repeats the pattern of delegation and coordination:

> First, it requests that a Pipe Path be set up between the storage tank and the cooking tank (event PP1: Reserve path).

> It then asks the Pipe Path to start any pumps on the path (event PP2: Begin pumping).

> When the required amount of juice has been transferred, the Juice Transfer asks the Pipe Path to turn off the pumps and then reports back to the Batch that the operation is complete (event B21: Transfer complete).

The Pipe Path object continues the theme of hiding information from the more intelligent object on whose behalf it is acting. Pipe Path attempts to reserve a contiguous route of pipes from the source to the destination (specified in terms of tanks). In order to isolate the path, it then closes all valves that are placed between a pipe that is in the path and a pipe that is not. It clears the path for the juice by opening all valves that connect two pipes in the path and finally opens the valves that connect the path to the two tanks.

Again, the Pipe Path state model does not know (or need to know) why it exists. It operates at the request of an object that has more knowledge and context: here either the Juice Transfer or the Canning Operation.

Layering on the OCM

By convention, the OCM is laid out with the most knowledgeable and powerful objects near the top of the page, and with less knowledgeable objects successively down the page. This provides a rough layering of the objects consistent with the paths of event communication required in the system.

Lowest layer. In the lowest layer we place objects with limited knowledge of the purpose of the system. These objects, like the Valve, simply respond obediently to events. Objects in the lowest layer correspond to servers in design terminology [2]. In real-time systems, such objects serve to hide the details of the signal interface to the hardware; they correspond to Parnas's virtual devices [3].

Highest layer. At the highest layer we place objects that incorporate the intention and purpose of the system, like the Batch object. These objects generate events to guide lower-layer objects through their lifecycles and receive events from below when a lower-layer instance has arrived at a significant state. Objects in the highest layer correspond to actors in the terminology of object-oriented design.

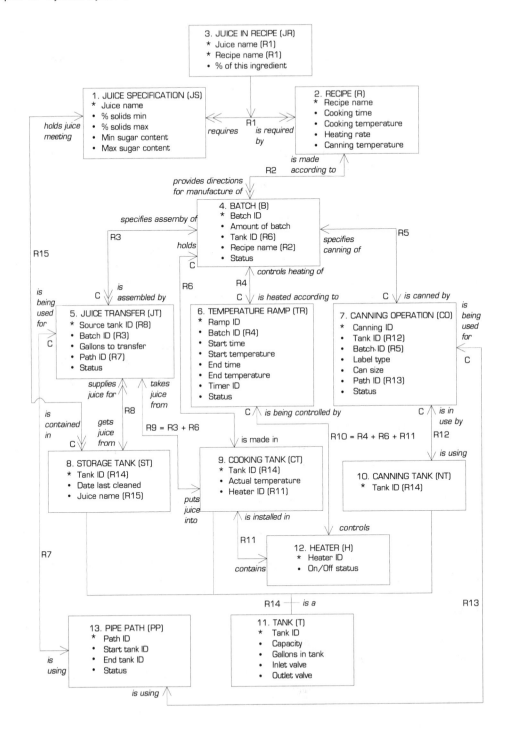

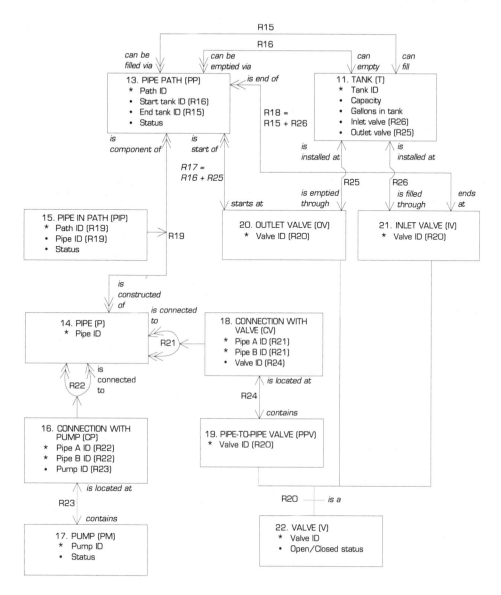

Figure 5.2.2: The information model for the juice plant. The diagram
has been split in two pieces for presentation here. The
Tank and Pipe Path objects appear on both parts of the
diagram.

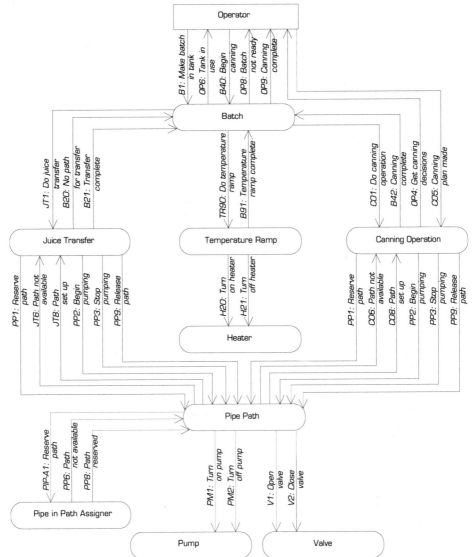

Figure 5.2.3: The object communication model for the juice plant.

Middle layers. The middle layers of the OCM are made up of objects related to suboperations, coordination of people or equipment, useful configurations of lower objects (like the Pipe Path), and role objects (like the Tank Inlet Valve). Middle-layer objects are sometimes referred to as agents, since they act on behalf of other objects: when a middle-layer object receives an event from above, it typically generates events to other objects below it.

5.3 Patterns of Communication

While any component on the OCM can, in principle, communicate with any other component, only a few communication patterns are commonly observed. To describe these patterns, we must first distinguish among various types of events.

Types of Events

An *external event* is an event that is generated by an external entity (terminator) and received by a state model in the system.   There are two kinds of external events:

> An *unsolicited event* is an external event that was not caused to occur by some previous action of the system. For example, B1: Make batch in tank is unsolicited: it is generated by the operator when he wants to make a batch. The system does not prompt the operator to do this, and therefore has no advance warning of the event's arrival.

> A *solicited event* is an external event that was generated in response to some previous activity of the system. For example, if a close command (event) is sent to a physical valve, the responding "valve is now closed" event is a solicited one.

An *internal event* is an event that is generated by a state model within the system.

Top-driven Pattern

In the top-driven pattern (shown in Figure 5.3.1), a top-layer object receives unsolicited events from operators (or similar intelligent external entities) to initiate significant operations for the system as a whole. In this situation, the top-layer object is likely to work like the Batch object, delegating work downward on the OCM by means of internal events. Both the top- and middle-

93

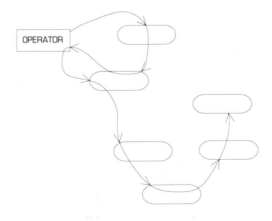

Figure 5.3.1: Top-driven communication on the OCM.

layer objects may prompt the operator for additional information as the processing continues; in this case, the top- and middle-layer objects will receive
solicited events that allow them to continue their work.

Bottom-driven Pattern

If an unsolicited event is directed at a bottom-layer object, the receiving object
typically has insufficient context to determine the appropriate response. It is
therefore likely that the bottom-layer object will add some information to the
incoming event data and generate an internal event upward. This pattern will
continue up the OCM until an object with sufficient knowledge and context is
reached. At this point it can be determined what needs to be done for the system
to respond appropriately, and the receiving object will then delegate the work
downward. This pattern is illustrated in Figure 5.3.2.

5.4 Threads of Control

Concept of a Thread of Control

A *thread of control* is the sequence of actions and events that occurs in response
to the arrival of a particular unsolicited event when the system is in a particular
state (see Figure 5.4.1). The thread of control is a conceptual entity with
meaning to the analyst: it describes what happens in the system if an unsolicited
event occurs when the system is in a particular state.

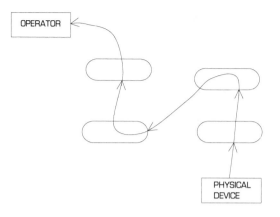

Figure 5.3.2: Bottom-driven communication on the OCM.

A thread of control may include activity outside the system: somewhere along the thread, an event may be generated to a terminator causing the terminator to execute some external activity. If the terminator responds with a solicited event, this event, as well as the external activity, are considered to be part of the thread of control.

If an action along the thread of control generates more than one event, the thread of control splits so that two or more legs of the same thread of control are active at the same time.

Termination of the Thread

Each leg of the thread of control eventually terminates. This can happen in one of three ways:

1. An action that generates no events is reached. The leg then terminates in this action, and no subsequent activity occurs along the leg.

2. An action that generates an event to a terminator is reached, and the terminator does not respond with a solicited event. In this case, the activity terminates outside the system.

3. An action that generates an event to release a controlled resource is reached. The leg then terminates in this action. Subsequent activity may now take place along another thread of control that was held up waiting for the controlled resource to become available.

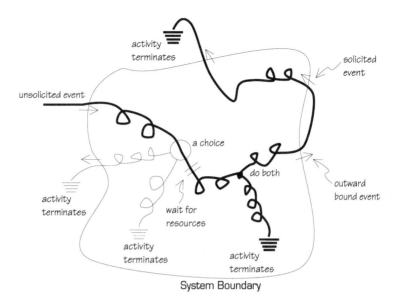

Figure 5.4.1: Conceptual sketch showing three threads of control. The highlighted thread is composed of two legs and a common segment.

For example, consider the Customer-Clerk problem discussed in Chapter 4 (see Figure 5.4.2). Suppose that there is only one clerk, who is currently busy serving customer 9, and that the Service Assigner is in state 1: Waiting for Customer. Then if the unsolicited event CS1: Customer Enters (customer 10) arrives, only the following actions are executed:

Customer state 1: Wait for Clerk
Service Assigner state 2: Wait for Clerk

The thread of control emanating from the unsolicited event is now temporarily held up until the clerk finishes with the previous customer, generating S-A2. As illustrated in Figure 5.4.2, the *generation* of S-A2 is considered to be a part of the thread of control that began with the arrival of customer 9, while the *transition* of the Service Assigner state machine from state 2: Wait for Clerk to state 3: Assigning is considered to be part of the thread of control having to do with serving customer 10.

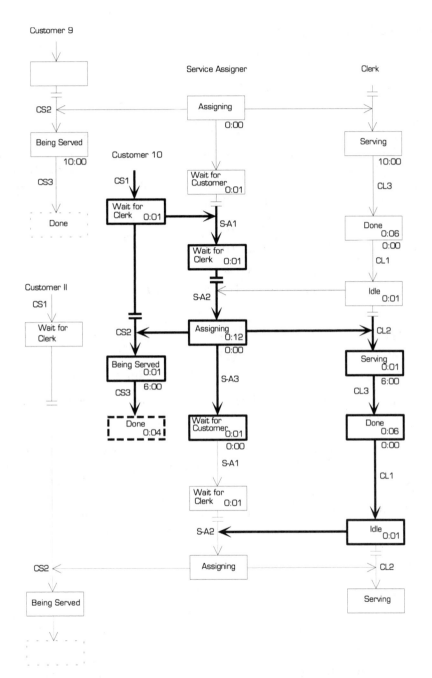

Figure 5.4.2: Thread of control chart for the Customer–Clerk problem.

Thread of Control Chart

Figure 5.4.2 provides an example of a thread of control chart: a graphical representation of the succession of events and states occupied by instances that participate in a particular thread of control. Each instance appears separately as the string of states it occupies as the thread progresses. The states occupied by a single instance are connected by arrows, each labeled with the event that causes the transition to the next state. If an instance generates an event to another state machine and that event causes a transition, an arrow is drawn from the state that generated the event to the transition of the receiving instance. The chart is laid out along a relative time axis, with the states placed on the chart in the order (top to bottom) in which they are occupied.

Time and the Thread of Control

The thread of control chart can be used to analyze the time it takes the system to respond to an unsolicited event. To discuss this in detail, we first need some terminology.

- The time an instance occupies a state is made up of two components: the action time and the dwell time.

- The *action time* is the time required to execute the action.

- The *dwell time* is the time the instance remains in the state after completion of the action.

Dwell time may be entirely determined by the instance and the state: it took ten minutes to serve customer 9 and six minutes to serve customer 10. Alternatively, dwell time may be determined by interactions between the state machines: the length of time Customer 10 needs to remain in Waiting for Clerk is zero, but the actual dwell time for this state may be considerably longer, depending on the availability of the clerk.

To portray the timing of the thread of control on the chart:

- Annotate each state with its action time.

- If the dwell time of a state is determined by the instance and the state alone, annotate the transition out of this state with the intrinsic dwell time.

- If the dwell time of a state is determined by interactions between state machines, place a capacitor symbol on the transition out of that state.

The time required to respond to the unsolicited event CS1 (Customer 10's arrival) can now be compiled from the chart. Since this thread of control splits into two legs, we compile the data in three parts.

Common segment. This portion of the thread of control begins with the arrival of CS1 and ends with the Assigner executing the action of the Assigning state. Assume that Customer 10 arrived when the clerk had been serving Customer 9 for seven minutes. Then time taken for the common segment is:

STATE MACHINE	ACTION	TIME COMPONENT	DURATION
Customer 10	Wait for Clerk	action time	0:01
Clerk	Serving	dwell time (remainder)	3:00
Clerk	Done	action time	0:06
Clerk	Done	dwell time	0:00
Clerk	Idle	action time	0:01
Assigner	Wait for Clerk	dwell time	0:01
Assigner	Assigning	action time	0:12
		Total	3:21

Left leg. The left leg of this thread of control begins with Customer 10 executing the action of the Being Served state, and ends when the customer completes the Done action. The time required for this leg is:

Customer 10	Being Served	action time	0:01
Customer 10	Being Served	dwell time	6:00
Customer 10	Done	action time	0:04
		Total	6:05

Right leg. The right leg begins with the clerk executing the action of the Serving state and ends with the completion of the Idle action. The time required for this leg is:

Clerk	Serving	action time	0:01
Clerk	Serving	dwell time	6:00
Clerk	Done	action time	0:06
Clerk	Done	dwell time	0:00
Clerk	Idle	action time	0:01
		Total	6:08

The total response time for the unsolicited event CS1 is then 9:26 for the response on the left leg and 9:29 for the response on the right.

Item Order

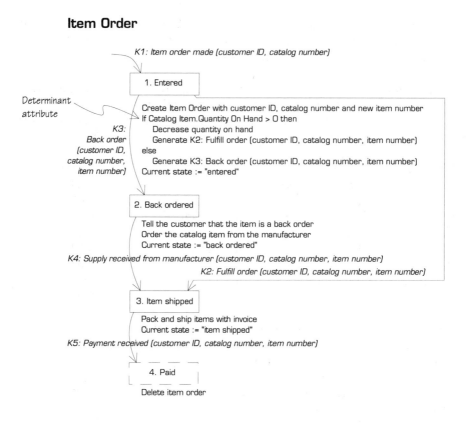

Figure 5.5.1: Catalog Item.Quantity on Hand is a determinant attribute, since it determines what events are generated by this action.

Applicability

The thread of control chart is most useful as a tool for understanding the interactions between a small number of instances. However, as the number of instances increases, it can become more and more difficult to achieve an intelligible layout of the chart; in addition, the chart can become unmanageably large. An alternative approach for understanding the thread of control is simulation: a technique that plays the state machine interactions out in time rather than in space, as on the chart.

5.5 Simulation

To be certain that the system as a whole makes an appropriate response to an unsolicited event, one can trace the thread of control by simulation. A three-step strategy is required:

1. Establish the initial state of the system.

2. Accept the unsolicited external event and play out the thread of control to see what happens.

3. Evaluate the outcome to see if it is correct.

Establishing System State

The complete state of the system is given by the values of all attributes of all instances in the system. For the purposes of tracing a particular thread of control, we must establish values for those attributes that affect the development of the thread. Such attributes are of two types: current state attributes, which determine what action is executed when an event is directed at a state machine, and determinant attributes:

> Definition: An action may contain logic such that the events generated by the action depend on values of attributes other than the current state attribute. Such attributes are known as *determinant attributes*, since they determine how a thread of control develops as it passes through the action (see Figure 5.5.1).

A systematic procedure for establishing the required attribute values is as follows:

1. Using the OCM and the state models, informally trace through the thread of control to determine what state models need to be considered and how many different instances of each object are required. Choose identifiers for the required instances and establish values for their current state attributes.

2. Inspect each state model involved in the thread of control to find any determinant attributes. Establish values for the determinant attributes.

3. Check to see how each determinant attribute is derived. If the determinant attribute is computed by state models involved in the thread of control, establish values for all attributes that contribute to the computation.

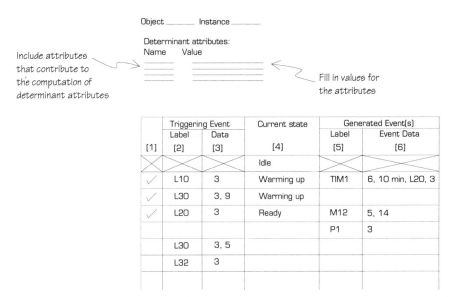

	Triggering Event		Current state	Generated Event(s)	
	Label	Data		Label	Event Data
[1]	[2]	[3]	[4]	[5]	[6]
╳	╳	╳	Idle	╳	╳
✓	L10	3	Warming up	TIM1	6, 10 min, L20, 3
✓	L30	3, 9	Warming up		
✓	L20	3	Ready	M12	5, 14
				P1	3
	L30	3, 5			
	L32	3			

Figure 5.5.2: A form for recording the progress of a simulation. Three events have been processed by this instance; two more are outstanding.

4. Verify that the attribute values chosen are consistent with one another: in the Customer-Account example, you would not establish an account with a current state of In Good Standing and a negative balance.

Executing the Simulation

Once the required attribute values have been established, we are ready to begin tracing the thread of control by means of a simulator. If you do not have access to an automated simulator, the clerical procedure described below can be used.

Figure 5.5.2 shows a form used to keep track of the entities that participate in the simulation. You will need one copy of the form for each state machine (object, Assigner, or timer) involved in the thread of control. Each terminator that participates in the thread of control will also require a copy.

Fill out the forms with the attribute values established previously.

Begin the thread. Take the unsolicited event that starts the thread of control and enter its label in column 2 of the state machine to which it is directed. Enter the event data in column 3.

Process the event. To process the event, examine the state model to find the appropriate transition, given the value of the instance's current state attribute. There are three possibilities:

1. If the event is ignored, write the name of the currently occupied state in column 4 of the row containing the event you are processing. Place a check mark in column 1 to indicate that this event has been processed.

2. If the event cannot happen, then we have found an error in some state model. Stop the simulation, repair the error, and try again.

3. If the event causes a transition, write the name of the new state in column 4. Then mentally execute the action associated with the state. Reflect any changes in the values of determinant attributes—either on this or on any other sheet—by recording new attribute values in the affected instances.

   Record the events (labels and event data) generated by the action in the columns provided for that purpose, using as many rows as required to record all the generated events.

   Finally, put a check mark in column 1 next to the label of the triggering event to indicate that you have processed it completely.

Propagation. Now, take each event that has just been generated and copy it into columns 2 and 3 of the state machine or terminator to which it is directed.

Select and process the next entry. Now pick the first unprocessed entry from any form. If the form is being used to track a state machine, process the event as described previously and do the subsequent propagation.

If the form is tracking a terminator, and the terminator does not produce an event, note the fact as "no events generated" in column 5. If the terminator produces a solicited event, write that event down as the generated event for the terminator. In either case, place a check mark in column 1 and propagate the event, if any, as described above.

Completion. The simulation continues in this manner repetitively:

- Pick the first unprocessed entry on any sheet,
- Process the entry, then

- Propagate the events or timer results if any

until all entries on all sheets have been processed. At this point the simulation is complete.

Evaluation

The results of the simulation are given by

- The final value of all current state attributes
- The final value of all determinant attributes (including attributes that contribute to the computation of the determinant attributes)
- The sequence of events that were directed to each terminator.

Evaluate the results to determine if (1) the attribute values are all consistent with one another and (2) the system produced the desired response as a consequence of receiving the original unsolicited event.

5.6 How to Think about Time

Interpretations of Concurrency

Most software practitioners think about time in two different ways, one based on our ordinary everyday experience and the other based on the way time is handled in a multitasking environment. The fundamental difference is concurrency: How does one interpret the idea that two things are happening concurrently?

OOA allows for two interpretations of concurrency. The *simultaneous interpretation* says that two things can be happening at exactly the same time, just as in the everyday world: I can be talking on the phone at exactly the same time that the letter carrier is putting mail into my mailbox.

The *interleaved interpretation* says that only one thing can be happening at any instant. To achieve the effect of simultaneous operation, two or more operations must be divided into suboperations and the suboperations executed in some manner deemed to be appropriate: First, one person involved in the phone conversation speaks, then the letter carrier inserts an envelope into the mail box, then the second person speaks on the phone, then the letter carrier inserts another envelope, and so on. This is the view of concurrency supported by multitasking operating systems.

OOA Time Rules

The OOA formalism makes certain statements and assumptions about time, hereafter called the *time rules*. Most of the time rules are exactly the same for both the simultaneous and the interleaved interpretations of time. Some rules must be stated slightly differently, depending on which interpretation of time you hold. The following presents the time rules for both interpretations, together with some discussion of the implications of the rules.

Rules about Actions

1. Only one action of a given state machine can be in execution at any point in time.

2. An action takes time to execute.

   On this issue, OOA takes a distinctly different perspective from many analysis methods that assume that actions take place instantaneously [4].

3a. Concurrency for the simultaneous interpretation: actions in different state machines can be executing simultaneously.

3b. Concurrency for the interleaved interpretation: Only one action can be executing at any time. Once an action gets control, it executes to completion without interruption. Actions from different state machines are interleaved with one another arbitrarily.

   In other words, the action is the unit of interleaving.

4. Once initiated, an action of a state machine must complete before another event can be accepted by the same state machine.

   It is the analyst's responsibility to ensure that the action will complete. Thus an action such as

   > Do forever
   >> If the temperature is too low, turn on the burner
   >> If the temperature is too high, turn off the burner
   > End do

   is not permitted, because

   - in the simultaneous interpretation of time, nothing more can ever happen in this state machine, since no further events can ever be received by the state machine.

- in the interleaved interpretation of time, once this action gets control, nothing more can ever happen in the entire system since events can never be received to make this action give up control.

Similarly, an action such as

> Do until Operator Request.Flag is set
> > If the temperature is too low, turn on the burner
> > If the temperature is too high, turn off the burner
> End do

is problematic. In the interleaved interpretation, this action will never complete (unless the attribute Operator Request.Flag is already set at the initiation of the action), because no other action can execute in order to set the flag that would allow this action to complete as intended. In the simultaneous interpretation, the action can complete, so the action is legal. However, it is unlikely that the physics of the situation actually requires that the heater be turned on and off as rapidly as the action implies. See Section 5.7 for a more revealing solution.

Rules about Consistent Data

1. When an action completes, it must leave the system consistent, either by writing data to paint a consistent picture or by generating events to cause other state machines to come into conformance with the data changes made by the sender of the event.

   Note that it can take time for the system to become entirely consistent under either interpretation of time. Even in the simultaneously operating real world, it can take time to propagate information so that consistency is achieved. For example, when you receive your bank statement, it is likely that the balance shown on the statement differs from that shown in your checkbook. This is due to the fact that it takes time for checks and deposits to arrive at the bank and to be reflected in the account's balance. The procedure you go through to verify the statement is correct takes care of this by accounting for uncleared checks and unrecorded deposits.

2. It is the responsibility of the analyst to ensure that the data required by an action is consistent, or that the action operates in such a way to allow for inconsistencies due to propagation time.

   We have already seen an example of this in the simple Customer-Clerk example. Recall that when the Service Assigner state machine entered state 1, it looked for a customer with state "Waiting for Idle Clerk" *and not appearing in an instance of Service*, for exactly this reason.

Rules about Events

1. Events are never lost: every event will be delivered to the state machine or terminator to which it is directed.

2. An event is used up when it is accepted by a state machine: the event then vanishes as an event and cannot be reused.

   This is analogous to most task intercommunication mechanisms in which a message cannot be received twice. Once the message has been received, it disappears as a message.

3. When an event is generated, it is immediately available to the state machine or terminator to which it is directed.

4. When an instance completes an action it is now in the new state. Then

   - (simultaneous interpretation) the instance will take an available event directed at it if any such events exist at this time.

   - (interleaved interpretation) at some indeterminate time after completion of the action, the state machine will accept a new available event if any such exist.

5. Multiple events can be outstanding for a given state machine.

   In the simultaneous interpretation of time, several state machines could be generating events to a particular receiver during the time the receiver was busy executing an action. This would cause events to build up waiting for the receiver to finish the action, at which point another event could be accepted.

   In the interleaved interpretation of time, several state machines can generate events to a particular receiver before the receiving state machine is allowed to accept an event and execute an action (because actions are interleaved arbitrarily). Again, this can cause multiple events to become outstanding for a single state machine.

6. If a state machine generates multiple events to a single receiving instance, the events will be received in the order generated.

7. If there are events outstanding for a particular state machine that were generated by different senders, it is indeterminate which event will be accepted first.

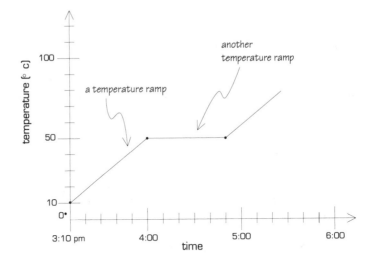

Figure 5.7.1: The Temperature Ramp object is an abstraction of requirements to hold juice at a constant temperature or to raise the juice temperature in a linear manner over time.

5.7 Repetitive Control

Many real-time applications require that certain data values be monitored and controlled actively and repetitively over an extended period of time. For example, in the juice plant problem of Section 5.2, there are requirements to raise the temperature of the juice slowly to the pasteurization temperature and then to hold the juice at that temperature for a prescribed time interval.

Either of these required industrial operations can be described as a line segment in a time-temperature graph, as shown in Figure 5.7.1. The operations are first abstracted as the Temperature Ramp object on the information model (see Figure 5.2.2). The dynamic aspect of the Temperature Ramp is given in the state model of Figure 5.7.2.

A higher-level object—in this case, the Batch—determines that a controlled heating operation is required. The higher-level object sends an event that causes an instance of the Temperature Ramp to be created. In state 1, the temperature ramp is created from the event data and the current temperature of the tank.

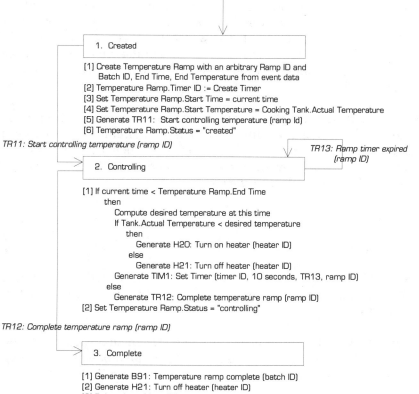

TR90: Do temperature ramp (batch ID, end time, end temperature)

1. Created

[1] Create Temperature Ramp with an arbitrary Ramp ID and
    Batch ID, End Time, End Temperature from event data
[2] Temperature Ramp.Timer ID := Create Timer
[3] Set Temperature Ramp.Start Time = current time
[4] Set Temperature Ramp.Start Temperature = Cooking Tank.Actual Temperature
[5] Generate TR11: Start controlling temperature (ramp Id)
[6] Temperature Ramp.Status = "created"

TR11: Start controlling temperature (ramp ID)   *TR13: Ramp timer expired*
                                                         (ramp ID)

2. Controlling

[1] If current time < Temperature Ramp.End Time
       then
          Compute desired temperature at this time
          If Tank.Actual Temperature < desired temperature
             then
                Generate H20: Turn on heater (heater ID)
             else
                Generate H21: Turn off heater (heater ID)
          Generate TIM1: Set Timer (timer ID, 10 seconds, TR13, ramp ID)
       else
          Generate TR12: Complete temperature ramp (ramp ID)
[2] Set Temperature Ramp.Status = "controlling"

TR12: Complete temperature ramp (ramp ID)

3. Complete

[1] Generate B91: Temperature ramp complete (batch ID)
[2] Generate H21: Turn off heater (heater ID)
[3] Delete timer (timer ID)
[4] Delete temperature ramp

Figure 5.7.2: State model for the Temperature Ramp.

The repetitive pattern of temperature monitoring and control occurs in state 2, in which the industrial operation is broken down into time slices: On each time slice, we check to see if we have reached the completion time of the temperature ramp. If the completion time has been reached, an event is generated to take us to state 3 and the completion of the ramp; otherwise the temperature of the juice is read and compared to the desired value, and the heater is turned on and off as required. Finally, a timer is set to cause re-execution of state 2's action on the next time slice.

Determining the Frequency

The frequency at which the action of state 2 is run is a significant analysis question that must be answered by application experts—in this case, the manufacturing engineers. The answer will take into account the amount of heat that can be delivered by the heater in any time interval, the specific heat and quantity of the juice, and the accuracy with which the actual temperature must track the specified ramp.

Finally, note that in any given problem one is likely to find that a number of different frequencies are required to keep different industrial operations under control. The analyst should ensure that each such frequency is specified separately. This will allow the system designers to determine how to package such operations into tasks and the code.

References

[1] Sally Shlaer and Stephen J. Mellor, "An Object-Oriented Approach to Domain Analysis," *Software Engineering Notes*, A.C.M. Press, New York, July 1989.

[2] Grady Booch, "On the Concepts of Object-Oriented Design," in Tutorial 5A for OOPSLA '88: *Specification and Design Methodologies in Support of Object-Oriented Programming*, A.C.M. Press, New York, 1988.

[3] D. L. Parnas, *Use of Abstract Interfaces in the Development of Software for Embedded Computer Systems*, Naval Research Laboratories Report 8047, Washington, D.C., 1977.

[4] Paul T. Ward and Stephen J. Mellor, *Structured Development for Real-Time Systems*, Yourdon Press, New York, 1985.

6

Process Models

All the processing that goes on in the system is stated in the actions. We now study in some detail the processing that makes up the actions.

6.1 Specifying an Action

Up to this point we have treated each action as a single unit of processing, placing most emphasis on what is required to drive the state models through their lifecycles: the acceptance and generation of events. We have been primarily concerned with the logic of each state model and of the system as a whole: when the various actions are executed with respect to one another, rather than the precise details of the processing within the actions.

At this point we focus our attention on the algorithmic or functional nature of the actions. The goal is to dissect each action into fundamental processes, which, taken together, define the required functional content of the system.

The primary tool used for this dissection is the action data flow diagram, a graphical representation of the internals of an action. We first present the action data flow diagram from a notational perspective. Then we discuss rules and guidelines for partitioning the action into processes, techniques for specifying the details of a process, and finally some additional work products useful in managing this aspect of the analysis.

6.2 Action Data Flow Diagrams

An action data flow diagram provides a graphic representation of the units of processing within an action and the intercommunication between them. The action data flow diagram is based on notation that was introduced and popularized in the late 1970s by Yourdon, Constantine, and DeMarco [1, 2] and later extended by others [3, 4, 5] to incorporate event-related concepts.

The action data flow diagrams of OOA are quite similar to those presented by DeMarco, with a few key exceptions:

- The Object and Attribute Descriptions document described in Chapter 2 is used in place of the traditional, alphabetically ordered data dictionary.

- In OOA, the problem is partitioned first into objects, then into actions, and finally into processes within an action, yielding at the bottom of this hierarchy a single flat data flow diagram for each action. This differs from traditional techniques that prescribe successive decomposition of function (alone) and produce a multilayered set of data flow diagrams.

- Control is represented on the action data flow diagrams, both explicitly through control flows and implicitly through certain data flows.

- Conditional outputs are explicitly represented.

Example. The Temperature Ramp object from Chapter 5 provides a compact example for demonstrating the notation of action data flow diagrams. The information needed to build the action data flow diagrams is contained in the information model (a portion of which is shown in Figure 6.2.1) and the Temperature Ramp state model (Figure 6.2.2). The events generated and received by the Temperature Ramp state model are shown in the partial event list of Figure 6.2.3.

Processes and Data Flows

An action data flow diagram (ADFD) for state 1 of the Temperature Ramp object is shown in Figure 6.2.4. This diagram represents the computation required by this action in terms of separate units of computation called *processes*. Each process is represented by a circle annotated with both a process identifier (to be discussed below) and a meaningful name describing the purpose or function of the process.

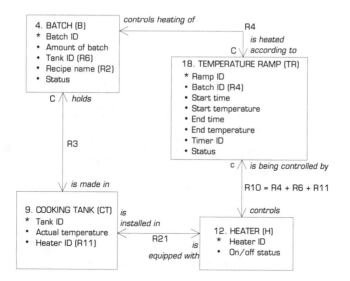

Figure 6.2.1: A portion of the information model for the juice plant.

Most processes require input data in order to carry out their functions and produce output data as a result. If a process requires input data, that data is shown being supplied to the process as a *data flow* directed to the process. If a process produces data as output, the data is shown as a data flow directed away from the process.

Persistent Data

Data that continues to exist after an action is complete is known as persistent data. Persistent data is represented on the ADFD as a data store, the logical equivalent of a table in a data base, a file, or a set of system variables. If a data store provides data to (or receives data from) a process, the data store and the process are connected by a data flow.

OOA uses three distinct types of data stores: an object data store, the current time data store, and a timer data store (to be discussed below in the paragraph headed Timers).

Object data store. The data that describes all instances of an object is represented as a data store labeled with the object's name. An object data store can be interpreted as a table containing values for all attributes of all the instances of the object, as discussed in Chapter 2. Alternatively, the object data store can be thought of as the instance data for all instances of a class in OOD.

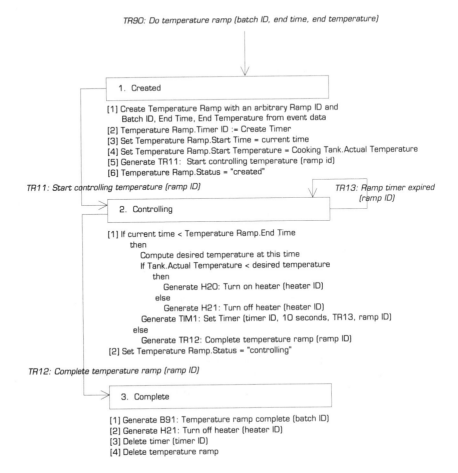

TR90: Do temperature ramp (batch ID, end time, end temperature)

1. Created

[1] Create Temperature Ramp with an arbitrary Ramp ID and
    Batch ID, End Time, End Temperature from event data
[2] Temperature Ramp.Timer ID := Create Timer
[3] Set Temperature Ramp.Start Time = current time
[4] Set Temperature Ramp.Start Temperature = Cooking Tank.Actual Temperature
[5] Generate TR11: Start controlling temperature (ramp id)
[6] Temperature Ramp.Status = "created"

TR11: Start controlling temperature (ramp ID)   TR13: Ramp timer expired
                                                              (ramp ID)

2. Controlling

[1] If current time < Temperature Ramp.End Time
        then
            Compute desired temperature at this time
            If Tank.Actual Temperature < desired temperature
                then
                    Generate H20: Turn on heater (heater ID)
                else
                    Generate H21: Turn off heater (heater ID)
            Generate TIM1: Set Timer (timer ID, 10 seconds, TR13, ramp ID)
        else
            Generate TR12: Complete temperature ramp (ramp ID)
[2] Set Temperature Ramp.Status = "controlling"

TR12: Complete temperature ramp (ramp ID)

3. Complete

[1] Generate B91: Temperature ramp complete (batch ID)
[2] Generate H21: Turn off heater (heater ID)
[3] Delete timer (timer ID)
[4] Delete temperature ramp

Figure 6.2.2: State model for the Temperature Ramp.

If a process reads attributes from (or writes attributes to) an object data store, the data flow connecting the process and the object data store is labeled with the attributes read or written. As shown in Figure 6.2.4, the <object name> part of the attribute's name may be omitted on such a data flow; that is, Tank ID (coming from the Batch object data store) is shorthand for Batch.Tank ID, the full name of the attribute. Similarly, Start Temperature (directed at the Temperature Ramp object data store) is short for Temperature Ramp.Start Temperature.

Current time data store. Data describing the current time is represented on the ADFD as a data store labeled Current Time. This data store can be interpreted

Label	Meaning	Event data	Source	Destination
B91	Temperature ramp complete	batch ID	T Ramp	Batch
TR90	Do temperature ramp	batch ID + end time + end temperature	Batch	T Ramp
TR11	Start controlling temperature	ramp ID	T Ramp	T Ramp
TR12	Complete temperature ramp	ramp ID	T Ramp	T Ramp
TR13	Ramp timer expired	ramp ID	Timer	T Ramp
H20	Turn on heater	heater ID	T Ramp	Heater
H21	Turn off heater	heater ID	T Ramp	Heater
TIM1	Set timer	timer ID + time to go + TR13 + ramp ID	T Ramp	Timer

Figure 6.2.3: Events generated or received by the Temperature Ramp state model.

as a system clock. The time data store is the source of any current time data needed by a process.

Data flows connecting the current time data store with a process are labeled with appropriately named variables representing the current time: day, month, hour, and so forth, or simply as current time.

Finally, in order to obtain a satisfactory layout of the ADFD, any data store may be replicated as many times as desired. It is understood that this is a matter of graphic convenience and all such copies of a data store refer to the same set of persistent data.

Received Events

The event that is received by a state model and so causes an action to be initiated is depicted on the ADFD as one or more *event data flows*: a data flow pointing into a process from nowhere. The event data flow is labeled with the names of the attributes that are carried by the event *and required by* the process. Thus, in Figure 6.2.4, the Create Temperature Ramp process requires access to all attributes carried by the event, while Find Tank for Batch requires only a single attribute.

Since, in the general case, an action can be initiated by any of several different events, event labels are not shown with the received event data.

115

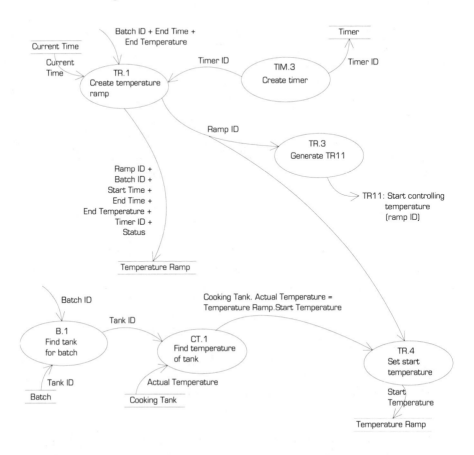

Figure 6.2.4: ADFD for state 1 of the Temperature Ramp.

Generated Events

If a process generates an event, that event is shown as a data flow directed away from the process. The data flow is labeled with the event's label, meaning, and event data, just as it appears on the state transition diagram or object communication model.

Process Identifiers

Each process on an ADFD is assigned to an object from the information model, according to guidelines to be given in Section 6.5. The object to which the process is assigned is reflected in the process identifier, which has the form <object>.<arbitrary process number>. <object> can be specified by either the

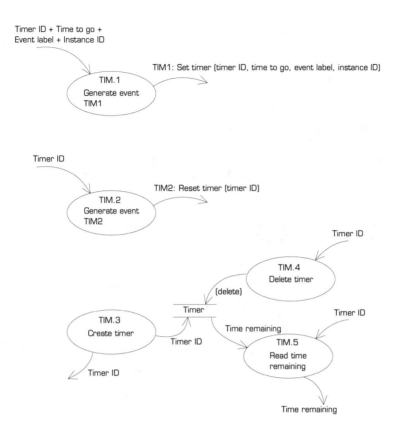

Figure 6.2.5: Processes that interact with the Timer object. The Timer data store represents the persistent data describing all timers in the system.

object number or the key letter assigned to the object on the information model. In the Temperature Ramp example, we have chosen to use the latter convention, so that TR, B, and CT indicate processes assigned to Temperature Ramp, Batch, and Cooking Tank respectively.

Data Flows between Processes

If data is produced by one process and consumed by another, a data flow is drawn between the two processes concerned. The data flow must be labeled with the name of the attribute(s) carried by the data flow. Note that it is common for an attribute on such a data flow to have two names: one based on the perspective of the process that produces the data flow and the other based on the perspective of the process that consumes it. This is illustrated by the data flow shown between processes CT.1 and TR.4 on Figure 6.2.4. The attribute carried by this data flow represents Cooking Tank.Actual Temperature to CT.1 and Temperature Ramp.Start Temperature to TR.4.

To save space on the ADFD, the <object name> part of an attribute's full name can be omitted if it can be deduced from the following rule.

> *Rule:* Any attribute produced or consumed by a process is assumed to be an attribute of the object to which the process is assigned unless otherwise stated.

Hence the attribute Ramp ID shown on the data flow connecting processes TR.1 and TR.4 is a shortened form of the full attribute name Temperature Ramp.Ramp ID.

Now consider the data flow between processes B.1 and CT.1. According to the rule above, the attribute carried by this data flow is both Batch.Tank ID *and* Cooking Tank.Tank ID. This is, in fact, exactly what is intended. From the perspective of the Batch object (and process B.1), the data flow carries the referential attribute Batch.Tank ID. From the perspective of the Cooking Tank object, it carries the identifier Cooking Tank.Tank ID.

Timers

To support the timer conventions described in Section 3.7, five processes have been defined as part of the OOA formalism. These processes, which are shown in Figure 6.2.5, can be used on any ADFD as required.

Deletion of Instances

If a process deletes an instance of an object, a data flow is drawn from the process to the appropriate object data store. The data flow is annotated as shown in Figure 6.2.6, the ADFD for state 3 of Temperature Ramp.

Control Flows

A control flow is a graphical representation of a constraint on the order of process execution. The ADFD makes use of two types of control flows: unconditional and conditional.

118

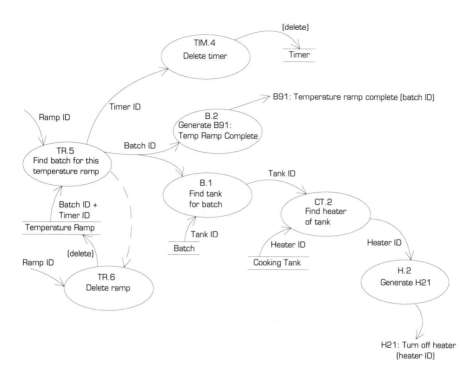

Figure 6.2.6: ADFD for state 3 of the Temperature Ramp.

Unconditional control flows. In Figure 6.2.6, an unconditional control flow (depicted as a dashed line) has been drawn from process TR.5 to process TR.6 to indicate that TR.5 must execute before TR.6. This is required to ensure that TR.5 is able to retrieve Temperature Ramp.Batch ID and Temperature Ramp.Timer ID before TR.6 deletes the instance.

Conditional control flows. In addition to providing a constraint on the order of process execution, a conditional control flow provides a graphical representation of the circumstances under which a process does (or does not) execute. Consider the process TR.7 (Determine if Ramp Complete) on Figure 6.2.7. Its purpose is to determine if the temperature ramp is complete by comparing the End Time of the ramp to the current time. Depending on the outcome of this comparison, either process TR.11 must execute or processes TR.12, TR.5, and TR.8 must execute. This requirement is represented by the conditional control flows shown on the ADFD. The fact that the control flow is conditional is indicated by the bar across it, as well as by the annotation that indicates the circumstances under which the flow is generated (and therefore the circumstances under which the receiving process(es) must execute).

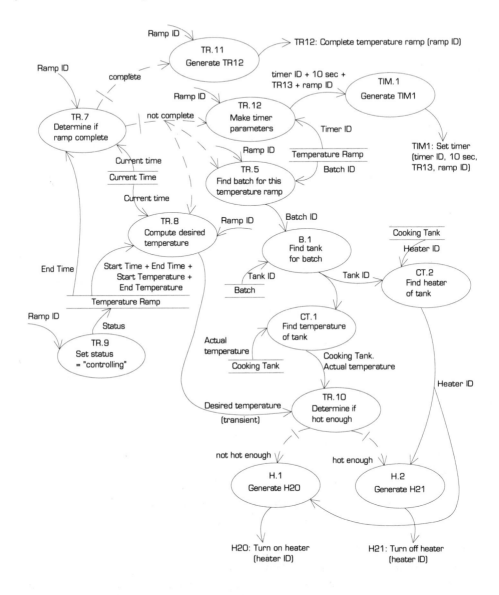

Figure 6.2.7: ADFD for state 2 of the Temperature Ramp.

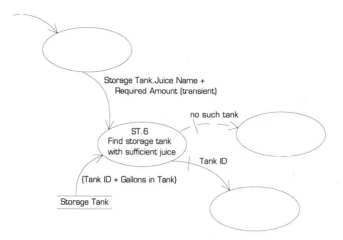

Figure 6.2.8: A portion of an ADFD for the Batch.

Transient Data

A process may produce data intended only for use by another process — that is, data that does not continue to exist once the action is complete. Such data is called transient data. If a data flow carries transient data, the data flow connecting the producing and consuming processes is labeled with an appropriate name and annotated to indicate that it carries a transient (that is, nonpersistent) data item. This notation is shown in Figure 6.2.7: the data flow between processes TR.8 and TR.10 carries transient data.

Multiple Instances

If a data flow can carry attributes for more than one instance of an object, the data flow is labeled with the names of the attributes enclosed in braces, as shown in Figure 6.2.8.

Conditional Data Flows

If a process produces data only under certain circumstances, the output data is shown as a conditional data flow: a regular data flow marked with a bar across it. The notation is illustrated in Figure 6.2.8 by the conditional data flow labeled Tank ID. This data flow is produced only if there is a storage tank that contains a sufficient quantity of juice.

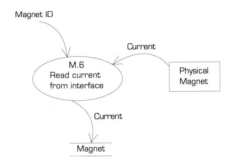

Figure 6.2.9: A process can read or write an entity external to the system.

External Entities

If a process reads data from an external entity such as a physical device, the external entity is shown as a terminator on the ADFD as shown in Figure 6.2.9.

6.3 Order of Process Execution

In general, there are some requirements on the order in which the processes of an action can execute. For example, in state 2 of the Temperature Ramp (Figure 6.2.7), process TR.5 must execute and produce the output Batch ID before B.1 can have the data it requires to proceed. The ADFD expresses requirements on the order of execution through the notion of availability of inputs. The requirements are cast as execution rules for an ADFD:

1. A process can execute when all its inputs are available.

2. Outputs of a process are available after the process completes executing.

3. Event data (attributes on event data flows) is always available.

4. Data from data stores and external entities is always available.

The execution rules support the following algorithm for playing through the execution of an ADFD by using tokens.

Start out by placing tokens on all data flows containing available data: all event data flows and all flows that originate in data stores and external entities.

Repeat until the action is complete:

If there is a process that has all its inputs available but has not already executed, "execute" the process by placing tokens on all its outputs.

If there is no such process, the action is complete.

Observe that the execution rules provide only a partial ordering for the execution of processes: for example, they do not prescribe the relative order of execution of processes CT.1 and CT.2 on the ADFD in Figure 6.2.7. The complete ordering is therefore left as a design decision; from an analysis perspective, it simply does not matter in which order CT.1 and CT.2 are executed.

When evaluating the order of process execution within an action, a control flow is treated like a data flow that carries no data. This can be made more explicit by restating two of the execution rules:

1'. A process can execute when all its inputs (including control inputs) are available.

2'. Outputs of a process (including control outputs) are available after the process completes executing.

6.4 Reuse of Processes

Because of the way in which processing is partitioned in OOA (first to state models and then to actions within a state model), it is very common to find the same process used in several ADFDs, either within a single state model or across several state models. When a process is reused in this manner, it should be labeled with the same process identifier and name wherever it appears on an ADFD.

Reuse Criteria

To verify that two processes are the same (that is, that the process is being reused in exactly the same form), check that both processes:

- carry out the same function

- read (or write) the same attributes from (or to) the same data stores

- accept, as input, the same attributes from sources other than data stores (that is, event data or data produced by another process)

- produce, as outputs, the same attributes to be consumed by other processes

- produce the same events as outputs

- produce the same conditional control outputs

Note that control inputs and unconditional control outputs are not pertinent in determining process reuse, since they only affect when (or the conditions under which) a process executes, and not the internal workings of the process.

These points are illustrated in Figure 6.4.1, in which

- process I is the same in both renditions (it does not matter where the input labeled x comes from as long as it is not from a data store),

- process II is different from I (since II obtains x from a data store and I does not), and

- process III is distinct from both I and II (because III writes the output z to a data store, whereas I and II do not).

What It Means to Be a Process

The requirements on reuse of processes are based on OOA's view of what it means to be a process. In OOA, a process incorporates both computation or transformation of data as well as any work required to read or write data from data stores. It is assumed that the process does not need to do any special work to access data that is supplied either from an event or another process; such data is considered to be analogous to the input parameters of a function in C or a procedure in Pascal. Similarly, outputs (other than those directed at data stores) are considered to be analogous to output parameters, in that the process does not have to do work to cause them to be taken away.

This view of processing and reuse ensures that if a process is reusable on the ADFDs it can be transformed into reusable code in implementation. This subject will be considered further in Chapter 9.

6.5 Forming and Assigning Processes

To build an ADFD from the pseudocode description of an action, the analyst must make numerous decisions as to which parts of an action to lump together into a single process and which parts to separate into different processes. Guidelines, based on the concept of a process type, have been developed to aid

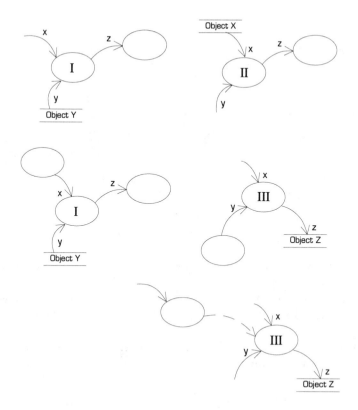

Figure 6.4.1: Processes I, II, and III are similar but distinct processes.

in making these decisions. These guidelines promote the creation of simple, highly reusable processes that can be mapped easily into a design, and most directly into an object-oriented design.

Process Types

The action should be partitioned to yield processes of four well-defined types:

1. Accessors

2. Event generators

3. Transformations

4. Tests

These types are characterized in terms of the purpose of the process and the use it makes of object data stores.

Accessors

An accessor is a process whose only purpose is to access data in a single object data store. The accessor may be any of the following:

Create accessor. A create accessor creates a new instance of an object. Process TR.1 of state 1 (Figure 6.2.4) is a create accessor.

Read accessor. A read accessor reads attributes of a single object. Process B.1 of state 2 (Figure 6.2.7) provides an example of a read accessor.

Write accessor. A write accessor updates attributes of a single object. Process TR.9 (Figure 6.2.7) is a write accessor.

Delete accessor. A delete accessor deletes an instance of an object. Process TR.6 of state 3 (Figure 6.2.6) is a delete accessor.

An accessor is assigned to the object corresponding to the data store it accesses.

Accessors are generally the most highly reused processes, both within the actions of a single state model and across the actions of different state models.

Accessors are analogous to OOD methods (published operations) that are (1) synchronously invoked and (2) perform in basically the same manner regardless of the lifecycle state of the instance addressed.

Event Generators

An event generator is a process that produces exactly one event as output. The event generator is assigned to the object to which its output event is directed.

An event generator does not access any object data store. Event generators are likely to be reused in several ADFDs.

An event generator is similar to an OOD method that (1) responds quite differently depending on the lifecycle state of the instance and (2) may be invoked synchronously or asynchronously, depending on the design.

Transformations

A transformation is a process whose purpose is one of computation or transformation of data: the process exists to convert its input data into a new form that is then output. Process TR.8 (Figure 6.2.7) is a transformation.

A transformation is assigned to the object corresponding to the state model in which it is embedded and may read or write the object data store of the object to which it is assigned. Hence process TR.8 is permitted to read the Temperature Ramp object data store.

Test

A process that tests a condition and makes one of several conditional control outputs is known as a test. Process TR.7 (Figure 6.2.7) is a test process.

A test is assigned to the object corresponding to the state model in which it is embedded and may read (or write) attributes of the object to which it is assigned.

Transformations and tests are typically most closely related to internal (private) methods in OOD.

When an Object Has Two State Models

When an object has two state models (a state model for the lifecycle of instances as well as an Assigner state model), it is useful to make a finer distinction, assigning processes not just to the object, but to one of the two state models associated with that object. Two forms of the process identifier are therefore required. When a process is assigned to the instance state model, its identifier takes the form

    <object key letter>.<arbitrary process number>

as usual. Processes assigned to the Assigner state model have identifiers of the form

    <object key letter>–A.<arbitrary process number>

Guidelines for making the individual assignments are the following:

- Accessors are assigned to the instance state model.

- Transformations and tests are assigned to the state model in which they occur (either the instance state model or the Assigner).

- Event generators are assigned to the state model that receives the generated event.

6.6 Naming and Describing Processes

Once processes have been formed, the analyst needs to state unambiguously exactly what each process does. This information is conveyed through the ADFD, the name of the process, and sometimes through a separate detailed process description. Guidelines for naming and describing processes make use of the four process types discussed previously.

Accessors

An accessor is named to state what it does:

> Create Temperature Ramp
> Find Tank for Batch
> Set Start Temperature
> Delete Ramp

If the process is quite simple, the process name alone is usually sufficient to specify what the process does. However, if an accessor contains some complex selection criteria, a process description will also be needed. Provide the process description in a straightforward narrative form:

> Process ST.6 (from Figure 6.2.8): Find storage tank with sufficient juice

> Description: Find a juice storage tank such that (1) the tank contains the specified type of juice, (2) the tank contains at least the required amount of juice, and (3) the difference between the required amount and the amount presently in the tank is a minimum.

> If there is no tank meeting requirements (1) and (2), return a control output; otherwise, return the value of Storage Tank.Tank ID that meets requirement (3).

Event Generators

An event generator is named Generate <event label>. Process descriptions are not required for event generators.

Transformations

A transformation is best named in terms of the data it produces: Compute Desired Temperature.

A process description is almost always required for a transformation. It can be cast in mathematical terms, in a narrative, or in a combination of the two. For example, Process TR.8: Compute Desired Temperature can be described by:

slope := (end temperature - start temperature) / (end time - start time)

Desired Temperature := slope * (current time - start time) + start temperature

Tests

Tests are usually named using "test" or "determine" followed by a name or phrase describing the condition or expression being tested, as in Determine If Ramp Complete (process TR.7, Figure 6.2.7). A process description is required if the expression being tested is defined and computed within the process.

6.7 State Process Table

A state process table provides a compact listing of the processes in the system and the actions in which they are used. Most analysts find this a useful tool during development of the ADFDs, both for maintaining consistency of names and process identifiers, as well as for identifying the reused processes in the system. A partial state process table is shown in Figure 6.7.1.

Note that the state process table can also be used to verify that the ADFDs are consistent with the object communication model: If an event is shown on the object communication model as being generated by one state model (call it state model A) and received by another (state model B), there must be a corresponding event generator in the state process table. The event generator must be used in some state of A and assigned to state model B.

It is recommended that the state process table be maintained in a CASE tool or spreadsheet so it can be sorted in various orders for the analyst's convenience:

- by process identifier (for checking consistency of process names and identifiers)

- by state model and action in which each process is used (for checking that each process on a given ADFD has been entered in the state process table)

- by process type (for checking consistency with the object communication model and for construction of the object access model).

State Process Table				
Process Identifier	**Type**	**Process Name**	**Where used**	
			state model	action
B.1	accessor	Find tank for batch	temp ramp	1,2,3
B.2	event generator	Generate B91	temp ramp	2
B.10	transformation	Compute amount of specified juice	batch	3
B.20	event generator	Generate B20	juice transfer	8
B.21	event generator	Generate B21	juice transfer	4
		. . .		
CT.1	accessor	Find temperature of tank	temp ramp	2
CT.2	accessor	Find heater of tank	temp ramp	2,3
CT.5	accessor	Set status = "connected"	cooking tank	2
		. . .		
H.1	event generator	Generate H20	temp ramp	2
H.2	event generator	Generate H21	temp ramp	2,3
		. . .		
TIM.1	event generator	Generate TIM1	temp ramp	2
TIM.3	accessor	Create timer	temp ramp	1
TIM.4	accessor	Delete timer	temp ramp	3
		. . .		
TR.1	accessor	Create temperature ramp	temp ramp	1
TR.3	event generator	Generate TR11	temp ramp	1
TR.4	accessor	Set start temperature	temp ramp	1
TR.5	accessor	Find batch for this temp ramp	temp ramp	2
TR.6	accessor	Delete ramp	temp ramp	2
TR.7	test	Determine if ramp complete	temp ramp	2
TR.8	transformation	Compute desired temperature	temp ramp	2
TR.9	accessor	Set status = "controlling"	temp ramp	2
TR.10	test	Determine if hot enough	temp ramp	2
TR.11	event generator	Generate TR12	temp ramp	2
TR.12	accessor	Make timer parameters	temp ramp	2
		. . .		
V.1	event generator	Generate V1	pipe path	3, 4, 6
V.2	event generator	Generate V2	pipe path	2, 5

Figure 6.7.1: Partial state process table for the juice plant.

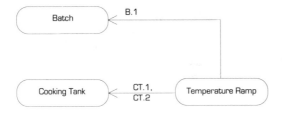

Figure 6.8.1: Partial object access model for the juice plant.

6.8 Object Access Model

Synchronous vs. Asynchronous Communication

In OOA, objects interact with one another both through events and through accessor processes. These two types of interactions have a different nature with respect to the time of their occurrence. When a state model generates an event, the target state model receives the event some time after the action in which the event was generated is complete. This communication is termed asynchronous. By contrast, when a state model accesses the instance data of another object through an accessor process, the data access takes place during the time that the action is running. This kind of communication is said to be synchronous.

The object communication model summarizes the asynchronous communication between state models in the system. The object access model provides the complementary view: a summary of the synchronous communication between state models and object instance data.

Representation

An object is represented on the object access model (OAM, for short) by a flattened oval labeled with the name of the object. The oval represents both the data describing the instances of the object (the object data store), as well as the state model, if any, of the object. If an object has two state models, two ovals are required: one to represent the instance data and state model and the other to represent the Assigner.

If a state model (call it state model A) makes use of an accessor assigned to another object (object B), an arrow is drawn from object A to object B on the

OAM. The arrow is labeled with the process identifier of the accessor. Note that all the information required to construct the OAM can be found in the state process table. Only accessor processes that are used by a state model other than that to which they are assigned need be considered. Figure 6.8.1 shows an OAM derived from the partial state process table of Figure 6.7.1.

6.9 Work Products

The work products of the process modeling phase are organized into documents as follows:

The Object Access Model. This is a one-page document containing the graphic representation described in Section 6.8.

Action Data Flow Diagrams. This document contains the action data flow diagrams for all the actions, ordered first by state model (using the state model's key letter) and then by state number.

State Process Table. This document contains three copies of the state process table: one sorted by process identifier, one by the state model and action in which each process is used, and one by process type.

Process Descriptions. The process description document is a compilation of any process descriptions produced, ordered by process identifier.

References

[1] Tom DeMarco, *Structured Analysis and System Specification*, Yourdon Press, New York, 1978.

[2] Edward Yourdon and Larry L. Constantine, *Structured Design*, 2nd edition, Yourdon Press, New York, 1978.

[3] Stephen M. McMenamin and John F. Palmer, *Essential Systems Analysis*, Yourdon Press, New York, 1984.

[4] Paul T. Ward and Stephen J. Mellor, *Structured Development for Real-Time Systems*, Prentice Hall, Englewood Cliffs, N.J., 1985.

[5] Derek J. Hatley and Imtiaz A. Pirbhai, *Strategies for Real-Time System Specification*, Dorset House Publishing, New York, 1987.

Domains

Up to this point we have discussed OOA as a tool for investigating and formalizing our understanding of the application domain — the subject matter of primary concern to the end-user of the system. Now we consider how OOA can also be used to develop precise definitions for those subject matters commonly associated with design.

7.1 Concept of a Domain

In building a typical large software system, the software developer generally has to deal with a number of rich and interesting subject matters: the application proper (such as railroad management, the juice plant, or the microwave oven), the interface to external hardware, the user interface, data management services of various sorts, purchased utility software (such as inventory control packages), and finally the operating system, programming languages, and development environment. This is clearly far too much material to deal with as a whole; consequently, we need a strategy for organizing these different subject matters throughout the software development process. The strategy we use in OOA relies on the concept of a domain.

> Definition. A *domain* is a separate real, hypothetical, or abstract world inhabited by a distinct set of objects that behave according to rules and policies characteristic of the domain.

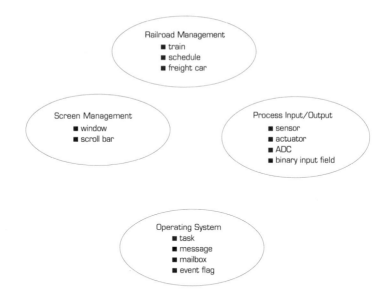

Figure 7.1.1: Some domains found in a typical real-time control system. Some prominent objects of each domain are shown for illustrative purposes.

Hence a Railroad Management domain is concerned with trains, tracks, and related equipment together with the operating policies governing their use, while a User Interface domain involves windows, displays, and icons together with an entirely different set of operating policies. Figure 7.1.1 displays some of the domains that might be required in a typical real-time system.

Each domain forms a separate and cohesive whole. In terms of objects:

- An object is defined in exactly one domain.

- The objects in a domain require the existence of other objects in the same domain: a train makes little sense without tracks to run on.

- The objects in one domain do not require the existence of objects in a different domain: trains and tracks can exist without windows or icons, and windows and icons can exist without trains.

The general principle of cohesion dictates that closely related ideas be kept together and unrelated ideas be kept separated. Since a domain represents a set of closely related objects, rules, and policies, it is treated as a unit for purposes of analysis: a separate set of OOA models is built for each domain.

7.2 Types of Domains

Domains are classified into four types according to the role each plays in the finished system:

- application domains
- service domains
- architectural domains
- implementation domains

Application Domains

The application domain is the subject matter of the system from the perspective of the end user of the system. This is the material that one normally thinks about in the context of requirements analysis: what does the user need this system to do?

For a given project, there is usually only one application domain. For the example of this chapter, we have chosen an application domain that is based on the real world: a Railroad Management domain. However, the application domain might be based on a much more abstract world: If the system to be developed were a CASE tool for OOA, the application domain would be that of the OOA formalism and would include objects such as Object, State, Event, and Process.

Service Domains

A service domain provides generic mechanisms and utility functions as required to support the application domain. Figure 7.2.1 lists a number of commonly encountered service domains together with the purpose of each. Note that, at analysis time, each of the service domains makes certain assumptions about other domains in the system. For example:

- The Alarm domain assumes that some other domain will supply information about trouble conditions when they occur. The Alarm domain doesn't have any knowledge of what these trouble conditions represent: they could represent failures in the operation of a railroad, failures in the juice plant, or failures in the hardware interface (PIO) equipment.

- The Alarm domain assumes that there is some domain available to deliver alarm displays of an appropriate type to the operator.

135

Process Input/Output (PIO)	Provides an organization of the signals composing the interface to the plant. Obtains sensor-based data and manipulates actuators as required by other domains.
Alarms	Collects notification of trouble conditions and anomalies. Presents such notifications to an operator for acknowledgement and possible corrective action.
User Interface	Presents and updates displays. Collects, correlates, and routes operator input from console devices.
Histogramming	Tallies data readings according to value. Prepares reports and displays of tallied data on request.
Trend Recording	Records successive values of selected attributes over a period of time. Creates displays of such recorded trend curves
History	Creates a permanent time-stamped record of all significant incidents in the operation of the industrial process and the computer system.
Data Archiving	Creates permanent time-stamped snapshots of specified datasets.

Figure 7.2.1: Typical service domains.

Architectural Domain

The architectural domain provides generic mechanisms and structures for managing data and control for the system as a whole. The objects in the architectural domain include abstractions of data structures and units of code. For example, in a pipes-and-filters architecture, a Filter (an object) would be described as a context-free process that transforms an input Character Stream into a related output Character Stream. This is very different from an object-oriented architecture, which would be described in terms of Classes, Published Operations, and Instances.

The architectural domain serves a number of purposes, each of which is discussed below.

Uniformity. The primary purpose of the architectural domain is to impose uniformity on the construction of the software. This is accomplished by stating policies covering:

- how data is to be organized and accessed
- how threads of control are to be managed

- how application and service code is to be structured
- what intercommunication is permitted between what units of code

These policies may be enforced by architectural components that operate at run time (such as a name server or event manager), by code generators or other code preparation aids, or simply by convention. In any case, the goal is to limit the complexity of the resultant system by providing standard structures and standard ways of accomplishing widely-needed functions.

System activities. Many systems require significant code to manage system initialization and shutdown, to maintain the capability of switching over to a warm standby system when substantial faults are detected, or to handle coordinated systemwide activities such as power fail recovery. These activities affect the entire system and cannot effectively be intermixed with the application or services. The architectural domain is therefore assigned the responsibility of providing such facilities for the system as a whole.

Portability. If the system being developed needs to run on multiple platforms and operating systems, the architectural domain can be defined so that applications and services interface only with the architecture and not with the operating system itself. In this configuration, the architecture serves as an isolation barrier, protecting the application and services from changes in the operating system, either from version to version or from platform to platform. Then when a new operating system is installed or the system is ported to a new platform, only the code in the architectural domain should require modification.

Performance measurement. If the architecture regulates control in a fairly direct manner, it may be practical to embed test points to make it easy to do certain kinds of performance measurements in the running system. For example, consider a system in which an architectural component (called the sequencer) causes several tasks to be executed in strict succession. The sequence is triggered repetitively, several times a second. Because the sequencer receives control both at the initial trigger and at the completion of each task, it can manipulate a DAC (digital to analog converter) so that the voltage appearing on the DAC tells you which task is running at any time. It is then an easy matter to connect the DAC output to an oscilloscope not only to see how long each task in the sequence is taking, but also to assess the stability of the timing.

Implementation Domains

The implementation domains include programming languages, networks, operating systems, and common class libraries. These domains provide the conceptual entities in which the entire system will be implemented. For example, suppose that the architectural domain has prescribed an object-oriented design based on classes. If the implementation is carried out in C++, the C++ class construct will undoubtedly be used to implement the architecture's idea of class; whereas if the implementation domain is Ada, an architectural class is likely to be implemented by a package constructed in a certain prescribed style. However, if the implementation language is FORTRAN, a class in the architectural domain will be rendered as a set of subroutines, each of which references a Common Block that has been labeled with a name unique to the class.

7.3 Bridges

Bridges, Clients and Servers

When one domain makes use of mechanisms and capabilities provided by another, we say that a bridge exists between the two domains. The two domains participating in the bridge play different roles with respect to one another and hence are distinguished by different terms: the domain that requires the capabilities is known as the client while the domain that provides them is termed the server. For example, in the Railroad Management system the application domain (as client) calls upon the Alarm domain (as server) to manage occurrences of trouble conditions; the Alarm domain (now acting as a client) in turn utilizes the User Interface domain (server) in order to maintain displays of current trouble conditions for an operator.

Assumptions and Requirements

During analysis, a bridge between two domains represents a set of assumptions (from the client's perspective) and a set of requirements (from the server's).

- The client thinks of the bridge as a set of capabilities that it assumes will be provided by another domain. The client does not care which domain provides the capabilities.

- The server thinks of the bridge as a set of requirements. The server does not care which domain needs the service, and therefore makes no assumptions about the client.

OOA mechanisms. The application and service domains assume that the mechanisms of OOA (data storage, event transmission, and the like) are provided in some form. This assumption forms a requirement for the Architectural domain: the Architectural domain must provide mechanisms for storing and retrieving data, for transporting events, and for operating timers. Note that the mechanisms need not be imitative of the OOA formalism; in Chapter 9 we will examine an architecture in which events are rendered not as asynchronous task intercommunication messages but as synchronous invocations.

Sensor-based attributes. The application domain assumes that sensor-based attributes such as Cooking Tank.Actual Temperature have up-to-date values. This requirement is assigned to the PIO domain.

Boundary-crossing events. When the OOA models of a client domain show that an event is generated to an entity outside the system boundary, it is assumed that there is a mechanism that can take the event and convert it into a form intelligible to the recipient. This constitutes a requirement for the PIO domain (if the event is directed at physical equipment) or for a service domain that communicates directly or indirectly with an operator: typically, the User Interface or Alarm domain.

Similarly, when the OOA models of the application domain show that an event is generated by an external entity, it is assumed that the PIO or User Interface domain can provide that event in a form interpretable by the application domain.

As indicated in Figure 7.3.1, client and server domains may have different views of the same event: the event may have one label and set of event data when viewed from the client's perspective and a different label and set of event data when viewed from the server. For this reason, we do not formally balance events that cross between two domains, but leave this as an issue for design, since resolution of the different views typically involves issues of data typing.

Counterparts. Although an object in one domain doesn't require the existence of an object in another, an instance of an object in one domain may have as a *counterpart* an instance of an object in another domain. For example, a train (in the Railroad Management domain) may have a counterpart train icon in the User Interface domain. The intention is that the train icon represent the train to the operator. Hence the position of the icon on the screen (screen coordinates) must be derived in some orderly way from the milepost position of the train in the real world.

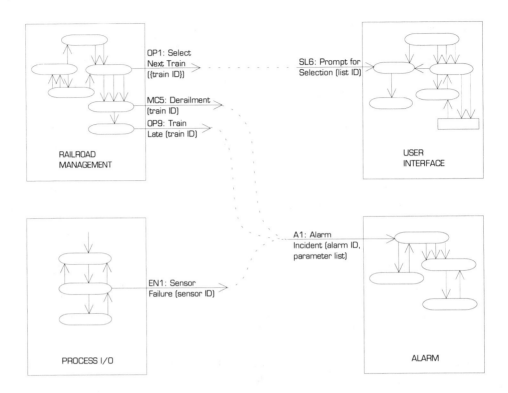

Figure 7.3.1: Client and server domains typically have different views of the same event.

This imposes a requirement on the User Interface domain: it must be possible to drive a display in which the position of an icon is derived from attributes of a counterpart instance in another domain.

7.4 Defining Domains

Domains

Identify the domains needed for the system before beginning construction of the OOA models. Give each domain a name and prepare a mission statement for each. The mission statement should provide a charter for constructing the OOA models for the domain. For example:

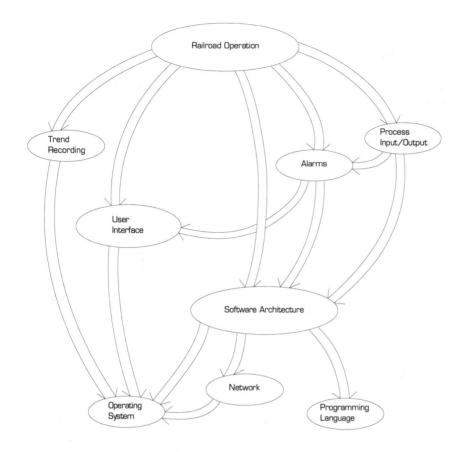

Figure 7.4.1: Domain chart for the automated Railroad
Management System.

Railroad Management: Schedules and monitors trains and freight ship-
ments; schedules and records maintenance for all rolling stock; operates
wayside equipment such as signals and switches.

Process Input/Output: Organizes and operates the instrumentation that
interfaces the computer to the sensors and actuators of the plant.

It is not necessary to write mission statements for implementation domains
since these are typically well-understood.

Bridges

Next, identify the bridges between the various domains. Describe the purpose of each bridge in terms of the assumptions held by the domain acting as client. At this stage in the analysis, only a very general description of the bridge is required:

> Railroad Management – Alarm: Railroad Management uses the Alarm domain to manage occurrences of railroad trouble conditions.

> Alarm – User Interface: The Alarm domain uses capabilities of the User Interface to present reports of trouble conditions to the operator.

Domain Chart

A domain chart can be drawn to provide a concise graphic representation of the domains and bridges required in a system (see Figure 7.4.1). By convention, the chart is laid out with the application domain at the top of the chart, the implementation domains at the bottom, and the service domains in between, so that the bridges generally point down the page from client (above) to server (below).

Testing Domains

To verify that the domains you have identified represent truly independently-existing worlds, examine the domain chart and mentally replace any questionable domain with another that has a similar mission but different objects (Figure 7.4.2). If the modified domain chart still makes sense, you have confirmed the independent existence of the replaced domain.

7.5 Using OOA with Multiple Domains

Order of Work

Construct the OOA models for the application domain first. The OOA models for lower domains can be constructed in any order so long as you make certain that you have unearthed the assumptions made by all of a domain's clients before you embark on the analysis for that particular domain. In effect, this says that the analysis must move down the domain chart from client to server, and that you should not analyze a domain that acts as a server until you have analyzed all clients for that domain.

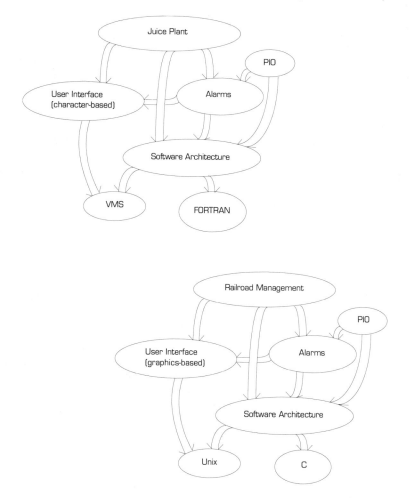

Figure 7.4.2: Testing domains by replacement.

Reporting Work

Despite the interest in alternative paradigms for software development, most projects (and especially large projects) are required to report their progress in terms of the traditional waterfall model consisting of work phases labeled analysis, design, implementation, and testing. If this is the situation for your project, we would make the following suggestions:

Analysis phase. Build the application OOA models for the analysis phase. If you want to make the analysis phase somewhat longer (or the design phase correspondingly shorter), include in the analysis phase the OOA models for the top-level service domains: those that have only the application domain as client.

Design phase. Assign to the design phase the work of building OOA models for the architectural domain as well as any remaining service domains.

Implementation phase. Assign to this phase all work required to convert the application, service, and architectural domains into code. Chapter 9 (and especially Section 9.10) offers some suggestions in this area.

8

Managing a
Large Domain

In this chapter, we consider techniques for managing the analysis of a large domain.

8.1 Concept of a Subsystem

While a small domain (consisting of fifty or fewer objects) can generally be analyzed as a unit, large domains must be partitioned to make the analysis a manageable task. To make such a partitioning, we take advantage of the fact that objects on an information model tend to fall into *clusters*: groups of objects that are interconnected with one another by many relationships. By contrast, relatively few relationships connect objects in different clusters.

When partitioning a domain, we divide the information model so that the clusters remain intact, as shown in Figure 8.1.1. Each section of the information model then becomes a separate subsystem.* Note that when the information model is partitioned into subsystems, each object is assigned to exactly one subsystem.

---

*If you are familiar with 2167A, think of a subsystem as a CSCI.

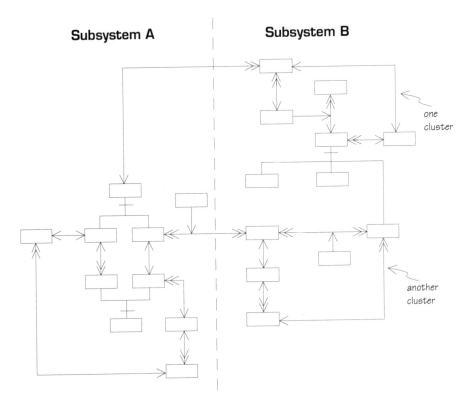

Figure 8.1.1: Partitioning a large domain into subsystems.

8.2   Initial Definition of Subsystems

The Bootstrapping Problem

Since the concept of a subsystem is based on partitioning the information model of the entire domain, we have a bootstrapping problem: in principle, we must have completed construction of the information model in order to partition the domain so that we can manage the work of building the information model in the first place. Because of this essential circularity, we have found it effective to develop an initial (usually fuzzy) definition of each subsystem before embarking on the construction of the information models, and then to use the resulting information models themselves as a precise definition of each subsystem in terms of objects. These definitions are then used to carry us forward into subsequent steps of the analysis and design.

Getting Started

Here are some suggestions for creating an initial definition for the subsystems of a large domain.

Object Identification Blitz. Identify as many candidate objects as you can by holding an object identification blitz: a community brainstorming session in which project members write down as many candidate objects as they can. This can frequently be done simply by general familiarity with the subject matter. If you have a preliminary project concept or requirements document, use this document as a source of ideas.

The blitz typically identifies only a small proportion of the objects in the domain. Fortunately, these objects tend to be very significant in the eventual information models, and they are likely to lie near the center of various clusters.

Next, sort the candidate objects into subsystems as well as you can, putting objects that seem to be closely related to one another in the same subsystem and assigning distantly related objects to different subsystems. In the process, discard any objects that belong to other domains.

User roles based on Objects. An entirely different approach is based on the concept of the roles played by the various users of a system. In the Railroad Management problem, for example, responsibilities for running the railroad may be divided so that one operator or department is responsible for maintenance of rolling stock, another group is responsible for the run-time operation of trains, and a third group takes responsibility for providing power to the trains using third rails or overhead cables. If the user roles appear to be associated with a distinct set of objects, then base a subsystem around each role: Rolling Stock Maintenance, Train Operation, and Electrification.

User roles based on time or function. In some situations, user roles are primarily based on the time that functions are carried out. For example, in a Battlefield Management application, different users could be associated with a planning phase, a battlefield operations phase, and a post-battle evaluation phase. Here, each of the phases deals with the same underlying subject matter — the same set of objects — but acts on the objects at different times. In such a case, do *not* base subsystems on the user roles since, for the most part, every subsystem would require inclusion of all objects in the system.

Producing the initial subsystem definition. The initial definition of a subsystem is produced in the form of a name for the subsystem, a description of the job of the subsystem (a mini-charter, similar in nature to the mission statement for a domain), and a list of objects tentatively assigned to the subsystem.

147

For the subsystem description, write a few sentences to outline the subject matter of concern to the subsystem. The description should emphasize the responsibilities of the subsystem.

> *Example* (not very good, describes subsystem in terms of objects): The Dispatch Trains subsystem is about schedules, holidays, routes, stations, and passenger loads under all anticipated circumstances.

> *Example* (better): The Dispatch Trains subsystem is responsible for computing schedules for all anticipated passenger loads, including normal commuting hour schedules, holiday schedules, and schedules that provide service for special events such as ball games, rock concerts, and Christmas shopping nights.

Final Thoughts

Establishing the initial definitions of subsystems is admittedly an intuitive operation. Interestingly enough, we find that most projects — even those new to OOA — do this quite well, even though the staff may have relatively little specialized domain knowledge to draw on. We therefore urge you to sketch the initial subsystem definitions quickly, taking at most a day or two for a large domain. There is little to be gained by agonizing over this matter, particularly since any misjudgments will be easily detected and corrected as the information models are constructed.

8.3 Analysis for a Large Domain

Once the initial definitions of the subsystems are in place, work can begin on the construction of the information models. Since the information model for a subsystem is most efficiently constructed by a small team (2 to 4 people at most), a large project usually has sufficient staff to allow several subsystems to proceed in parallel. Here are some issues and concerns that are likely to emerge during this process.

Unique Identification of Model Elements

To ensure that all objects in the domain have unique numbers and key letters and that all relationships have been assigned unique identifiers, it is wise to establish project-wide numbering conventions at the beginning of the analysis. A suggested convention is this: Assign each subsystem a special prefix letter and a range of numbers:

Subsystem A

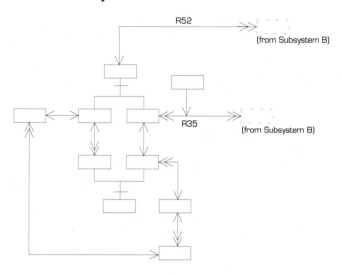

Figure 8.3.1: An inter-subsystem relationship can be depicted on the information models of both subsystems.

SUBSYSTEM	PREFIX	RANGE
Dispatch Trains	DT	1-99
Train Operation	TO	101-199
Track Management	TM	201-299

Then give each object and relationship in a particular subsystem a number chosen from the range assigned to that subsystem. Give each object a key letter that begins with the prefix letter assigned to the object's subsystem.

Inter-subsystem Relationships

An inter-subsystem relationship (sometimes called a spanning relationship) is one that associates objects in different subsystems. Assign such a relationship to the subsystem of one of the participating objects, and document it in the Relationship Descriptions document of that subsystem.

An inter-subsystem relationship may be shown on the graphical models of both the subsystems involved, as shown in Figure 8.3.1. To depict such a relationship on the information model for subsystem A, import the participating object from subsystem B. Annotate the imported object with the name of the subsystem to which it is assigned.

Duplication of Objects

Since the initial subsystem definitions do not provide any real guidance as to where one subsystem leaves off and the next one begins, it is quite possible that two teams working on adjacent subsystems will wander into one another's territory and produce models that have some number of objects in common. To protect against this, keep an eye on the models of nearby subsystems and assign any duplicated object to the subsystem with which it is most closely connected.

When searching for duplicates, keep in mind that the analysts working on the various subsystems may hold slightly different perspectives. As a result, a duplicated object may appear with different names or attributes in different subsystems. Compare the object description of any suspected duplicates. If you find that the object descriptions are basically referring to the same conceptual entity, negotiate a common name for the object and define attributes as required by all the subsystems. Assign the object to one subsystem only.

Split Clusters

If you find a number of inter-subsystem relationships defined between the same two subsystems, it may be the case that a cluster has been split. To investigate this problem, build a quick sketch model that includes the inter-subsystem relationships and the objects involved in them. Use the sketch model to determine how to reassign the objects to keep the clusters intact and to minimize the number of inter-subsystem relationships.

Unmanageably Large Subsystems

When an information model contains so many objects that the analysts working on the subsystem find it difficult to keep all of the model in their minds at once, the subsystem should be split into two. Examine the information model as it stands to see if the subsystem can be divided in a natural way without disrupting too many relationships. If so, try writing subsystem descriptions for the proposed new subsystems. If you can split the responsibilities of the original subsystem reasonably well, partition it into new, smaller subsystems.

If you cannot partition the subsystem without doing major violence to the information model, put this subsystem on a slower schedule and assign it to the most patient analysts. As the remainder of the subsystems are analyzed, you may be able to nibble off some objects near the subsystem boundary and assign them to neighboring subsystems (though this rarely helps much).

Adjusting Subsystem Names and Descriptions

If reassignment of objects causes the focus of the subsystems to shift during the course of the analysis, it may be appropriate to adjust the subsystem names or descriptions to match. The need for this kind of adjustment normally arises during construction of the information models; once these are complete you can regard subsystem names and descriptions as final.

8.4 Domain-Level Models

Three diagrams have been defined to provide an integrated top-level view of a domain in terms of subsystems. These diagrams — the subsystem relationship model, the subsystem communication model, and the subsystem access model — form the top of the documentation hierarchies involving objects and relationships, asynchronous (event) communication, and synchronous data access, respectively (Figure 8.4.1).

The domain-level models are very similar to one another in appearance. Each subsystem is represented on all three models as a box labeled with the name of the subsystem, the subsystem's prefix letter, and the number range for objects and relationships in the subsystem. It is recommended that the domain-level models be laid out identically so that they can be superimposed on one another via transparencies to provide a complete view of all the interactions between the subsystems.

Subsystem Relationship Model

A subsystem box on the subsystem relationship model (SRM) represents the entire information model for that subsystem. Depict any inter-subsystem relationships by a line connecting the two subsystems on the SRM. The line is labeled with the identifiers of the inter-subsystem relationships as shown in Figure 8.4.2.

Subsystem Communication Model

A subsystem box on the subsystem communication model (SCM) represents an object communication model for a particular subsystem. If a state model in one subsystem generates an event that is received by a state model in another subsystem, draw an arrow from the subsystem in which the event is generated to the subsystem that receives the event. Label the arrow with the identifier of the event(s) and, if there is sufficient space on the diagram, with the meaning of the event, as shown in Figure 8.4.3.

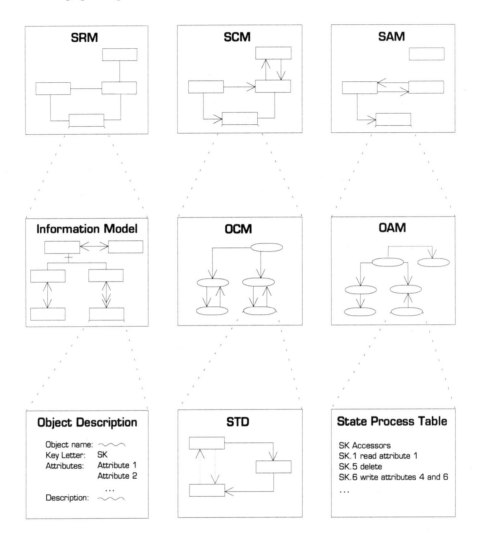

Figure 8.4.1: The domain level models form the tops of the hierarchies describing the information content of objects, asynchronous (event) communication, and synchronous data access.

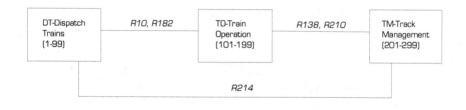

Figure 8.4.2: Subsystem relationship model for the Railroad
Operation domain.

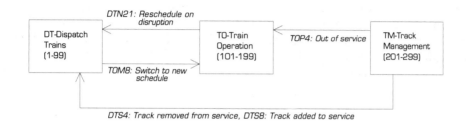

Figure 8.4.3: Subsystem communication model for the Railroad
Operation domain.

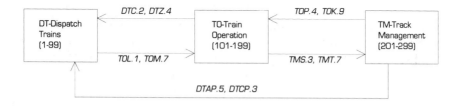

Figure 8.4.4: Subsystem access model for the Railroad
Operation domain.

Subsystem Access Model

A subsystem box on the subsystem access model (SAM) represents an object access model for one of the subsystems in the domain. If a state model in one subsystem (subsystem A) makes use of an accessor process assigned to an object in another subsystem (subsystem B), draw an arrow from subsystem A to subsystem B. Label the arrow with the identifiers of the accessors as shown in Figure 8.4.4.

8.5 Project Matrix

What the Project Matrix Represents

The project matrix [1] is a simple representation of the planning and organizational framework provided by the subsystems and by OOA. In the project matrix (Figure 8.5.1), each row of the matrix represents a step in the OOA method and each column represents a subsystem. The boxes formed by the intersection of rows and columns represent separate units of work to be accomplished. As a result, you can associate a number of items of information with any given box:

- The staff members who are assigned to do the work represented by the box

- The work products that are to be produced as a result of doing the work

- The amount of effort estimated to be required to do the work

- Current status of the work: complete, in progress, to be done

- The dates on which the work is expected to begin and end*

- The amount of effort that was actually required to do the work

Because the project matrix provides a compact and integrated view of the project's plans and status, many projects maintain a large copy of the project matrix fully annotated with the above information on a blackboard or poster to keep everyone up to date on the progress being made.

---

*When building the schedule for the project, use the boxes from the project matrix as the units of work to be scheduled.

Figure 8.5.1: Project matrix for the Automated Railroad Management System.

Analysis Activities

Up to this point we have placed most of the emphasis on the work products of OOA: what they are and what rules must be observed to ensure their consistency. This section presents an alternative view: OOA as a process that includes analysis activities required to support the formal models. The process is described in the framework given by the project matrix.

Information model row. The work associated with a box in the information model row breaks down into several distinct activities:

- research
- model development
- integration
- review

Research. The first task facing the analyst is to collect and assimilate pertinent information about the real (or hypothetical) world under analysis. Much of this information may be available in documents, both in general works available from libraries as well as in specialized works issued and maintained by the customer's organization: operations and policy manuals, engineering drawings and documents, data sheets, photographs, training materials, and the like. Additional information may need to be obtained directly from representatives of the customer's organization, people who are expected to perform as operators of the system, and various subject matter experts.

During the research phase, the analyst can easily become overwhelmed with information, only some of which is pertinent to the analysis. The most effective approach we have found for dealing with this is the classical engineering note: a short single-topic technical note or memo. To assimilate and condense the information that must be considered for building the information model, record each interview or collection of relevant findings from documents in a technical note.

Model development. Once you have a reasonably good understanding of the subject matter, work can begin on construction of the formal models. Start by sketching a first draft of the graphical information model. Fill in attributes and relationships as suggested by the technical notes.

As soon as you have a fairly complete draft of the graphical information model, begin preparing the object and attribute descriptions. This activity may raise additional questions for research and resolution. Continue improving the model and researching questions as they arise until all details are resolved.

It is not uncommon to reach the point where you have a few fundamental questions that simply cannot be resolved quickly since they depend on decisions yet to be made by the customer or by another department in your organization. In this case, you may have to suspend work on the particular subsystem until answers can be obtained. Alternatively, the best course may be to continue by preparing a technical note documenting the options. Then select one of the options, document your selection as an assumption in the document entitled Context for Review of Subsystem (as described in Section 8.6), and proceed with the analysis. While this strategy carries with it the risk of having to rework parts of the analysis later, it is likely to facilitate the decision-making process, since the complete analysis will reveal any implications of the option you have chosen to explore (and may shed some light on the other options as well).

Integration. Once the information model and associated textual documents are complete, build (or update) the subsystem relationship model for the domain in which the subsystem is contained.

Review. Because the information model is the foundation for all the analysis and design still to come, we conduct a detailed technical review of the work at this point. The goals of this review are two: (1) to verify that the pertinent aspects of the real world have been captured accurately in the formal models, and (2) to check that the model conforms to the rules of OOA: every object has an identifier, all relationships have been formalized and described, and so on. The review board should therefore include both subject-matter experts (to support the first goal) and modeling experts (to ensure the second). If you cannot provide subject matter experts for this review, substitute analysts who have not worked on this particular model. Supply the analyst-reviewers with the technical notes, which can then be used as the description of reality against which to review the model.

State models row. The activities associated with a box in the state model row are model development, verification of interactions, integration, and review.

Model development. Begin the state model work by sketching a rough object communication model to establish the layering of the objects as described in Chapter 5. Then build the state models (STDs and STTs) one by one and accumulate the event list as you go. It may be necessary to do some supplementary research to determine the fine points of behavior of various objects; if so, be sure to record your findings in technical notes.

In the process of building the state models, you will probably identify a few additional attributes that need to be added to the information model. To save work, keep a list of these modifications and update the information model all at once when the state models are complete.*

Verification of interactions. If the interactions between the state models are not easily understood from the STDs and the object communication model alone, play through the interactions using an automated simulator or the manual procedure described in Chapter 5. Alternatively, depict the interactions on a thread of control chart. In any case, be prepared to explain the interactions of the various state models at the review for this box.

Integration. Once the state models and object communication model are complete, build (or update) the subsystem communication model for this domain.

Review. In reviewing the work products of a box in the state model row, place the emphasis equally on (1) evaluating whether or not the operation of the real world has been correctly captured and (2) verifying the consistency of the state models, object communication model, and subsystem communication model.

---

*To make it easier to correlate the information model with the state models, many analysts take this opportunity to adjust the layout of the information model so that it matches the layout of the object communication model.

Process models row. The work associated with a box in the process models row requires three activities: model development, followed by the usual integration and review. This work is quite straightforward and generally proceeds very rapidly.

Model development and integration. Divide the work so that each analyst is responsibile for producing the ADFDs for some number of state models. While this work is in progress, each analyst can maintain a separate state process table. When the ADFDs are complete, merge the separate state process tables and resolve any discrepancies in process names and identifiers. Then produce the object access model for the subsystem and update the subsystem access model for the whole domain.

Review. The review for the process models box should verify that the actions of the state models have been accurately transcribed into ADFDs. Since no new subject-matter information enters the analysis at this step, the verification is best performed by analysts.

8.6 Subsystem Notebook

To support the needs of both analysts and reviewers of a subsystem, we recommend that a separate subsystem notebook be created for each subsystem or small domain. The subsystem notebook contains the work products of OOA, packaged more or less "down the column" of the project matrix. Figure 8.6.1 shows the table of contents for a typical subsystem notebook.

Part 1 of a subsystem notebook provides a context for understanding and review of the detailed subsystem-specific material to follow. Note that, with the exception of items 1.1 and 1.5, the documents in Part I are identical for all subsystems, and could therefore be removed to a separate domain notebook.

Assuming that the subsystem notebook is the packaging used for significant formal reviews involving the customer,* we have reserved the first position in the notebook for a message to the reviewers. The contents and level of formality of this document are highly dependent on the conditions under which the

---

*If you need to produce review documents in some alternative form (such as that required by 2167A), repackage the material in the subsystem notebook after you have completed the process models for the subsystem. We believe this is actually more efficient that trying to produce the alternative packaging directly.

<xyz> Subsystem Notebook

Table of Contents

Part 1: Subsystem Context

1.1 Context for Review of Subsystem <xyz>
1.2 Domain Chart
1.3 Missions and Bridge Descriptions
1.4 Project Matrix
1.5 <xyz> Subsystem Description
1.6 Subsystem Relationship Model
1.7 Subsystem Communication Model
1.8 Subsystem Access Model

Part 2: Information Model

2.1 <xyz> Information Model
2.2 <xyz> Object and Attribute Descriptions
2.3 <xyz> Relationship Descriptions

Part 3: State Models

3.1 <xyz> Object Communication Model
3.2 <xyz> State Models
3.3 <xyz> Event List

Part 4: Process Models

4.1 <xyz> Object Access Model
4.2 <xyz> State Process Table
4.3 <xyz> Action Data Flow Diagrams
4.4 <xyz> Process Descriptons

Appendices

AA. Loose Ends List
A.   (various technical notes, simulation results, other detailed items)
B.
C.

Figure 8.6.1: Table of Contents for a subsystem notebook.

system is being developed. On past projects, we have used this first document to familiarize the reviewer with OOA, to alert the customer to problems encountered in collecting information from his organization, and to record major assumptions on which the project is based ("We have assumed that the such-and-such sensors will be installed and operational prior to system deployment.")

Parts 2, 3 and 4 of the notebook contain the standard OOA work products. Should you wish to include thread of control charts, insert them as item 3.4. Results of simulation runs, being extremely detailed, are probably better packaged as appendices.

The last section of the subsystem notebook is reserved for detailed material providing backup for the formal OOA models. Include here any particularly significant technical notes*, data sheets, and the like. Finally, note the first item in the list of appendices: the Loose Ends List. We use this document as a place to record outstanding questions, minor corrections to be made ("Platform.Passenger Station is referential and should be marked as (R8) on the graphical model"), and similar items that are still to be resolved. The Loose Ends List is typically updated every week or two while the analysis is in progress. Since it is an internal working document, you may want to remove it from the notebook and table of contents prior to formal review.

References

[1] Sally Shlaer, Diana Grand, and Stephen J. Mellor, "The Project Matrix: A Model for Software Engineering Project Management," *Proceedings of the Third Software Engineering Standards Application Workshop (SESAW III)*, I.E.E.E. Computer Society Press, Silver Spring, MD, 1984.

---

*For day to day reference, we generally file all technical notes in a separate notebook, and bring forward into the Subsystem Notebook only those key results appropriate for formal review.

Transforming Object-Oriented Analysis into Object-Oriented Design

In this chapter we present a transformation of OOA into an object-oriented design. The design is represented in the OODLE notation, which is described in Appendix A. If you are unfamiliar with object-oriented design concepts or with the OODLE notation, we suggest that you read the appendix before embarking on this chapter.

9.1 Background

This chapter presents a particular object-oriented design that is derived in a very direct manner from the models of an object-oriented analysis. This design is not the only possible object-oriented design that can be so derived; rather, it represents a basic synchronous design that can be extended, elaborated, and adjusted to accommodate size and performance constraints as required.

Design Approach

More interesting than the design itself is the approach. In the description to come, note the prominence of the architectural domain:

- Mechanisms supporting state machines and timers are provided by classes in the architectural domain.

- Policies and conventions for producing the application design are laid down by the architectural domain. These conventions are expressed as

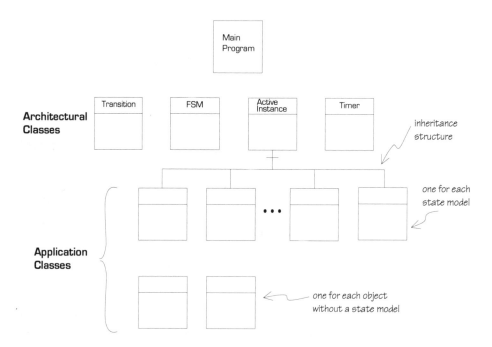

Figure 9.2.1: Program components prescribed by this architecture.

transformation rules that generate components of the design from components of the OOA models.

These two points, the hallmarks of Recursive Design [1], ensure that the system is designed and implemented in a uniform and coherent manner. In addition, the transformation rules allow you to move directly to the final design of the application classes. Experience indicates that this is especially important for large projects: the notion of iterating a design over hundreds of classes is clearly an impractical fantasy, despite the current popularity of the idea.

Terminology

The terminology used in the object-oriented literature today varies significantly from author to author depending, at least in part, on terms defined in the (still evolving) object-oriented programming languages. In this chapter, we shall use the following language-independent terms in addition to those defined in Appendix A.

object	an abstraction of a real-world thing; an object as in OOA; a typical but unspecified instance
instance	a single specified instance of a class; a specified instance of an analysis object
constructor	an operation that creates an instance of a class
handle	a pointer or other reference to the data structure containing data describing an instance
instance component	a logical component that is implemented as a separate element of the instance's data structure. The analogue of an element of member data in C++.

9.2 Overview of the Design

The design of the system as a whole is expressed in terms of the design of a single program (an Ada or VMS task or a Unix® process). Consistent with the development of object-oriented technology today, it is assumed that if there are multiple programs in the system, communication between them is a relatively minor matter; hence this subject is not addressed by this architecture.*

As shown in Figure 9.2.1, each program in the system is made up of

- a main program
- four architectural classes
- some number of application classes.

The main program is responsible for dealing with any intertask communication required (by messages or rendezvous) and for invoking operations of the application classes to initiate threads of control. In addition, the main program must initialize the application classes before any of the true work is undertaken.

Three architectural classes — Finite State Model, Transition, and Active Instance — supply mechanisms required to initialize and traverse state machines. The fourth architectural class, Timer, provides a mechanism analogous to the Timer object of OOA.

---

*But note that in a large multitasking application, intertask communication is a significant determinant of the complexity and performance of the system, and is therefore likely to be severely regulated by the architecture.

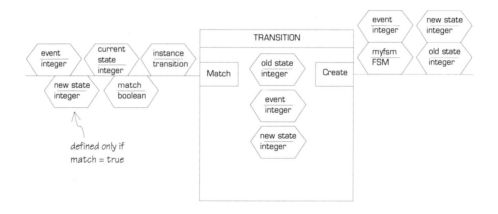

Figure 9.3.1: Class Diagram for the Transition Class.

The application classes are analogous to and derived from the objects and state models of OOA. Each one is responsible for the same activities carried out by its OOA analogue.

9.3 The State Machine Mechanism of the Architecture

The state machine mechanism of the architecture is provided in three architectural classes: Transition, Finite State Model (or FSM, for short) and Active Instance.

Encapsulated Data

The Transition class (see Figure 9.3.1) encapsulates data describing each transition for all state models in the program. Each instance of Transition corresponds to a cell (other than a "can't happen" cell) in a state transition table.

- If the cell is a "new state" cell, the instance variable new state has as its value the state number found in the cell.

- If the cell is an "event ignored" cell, the new state is zero.

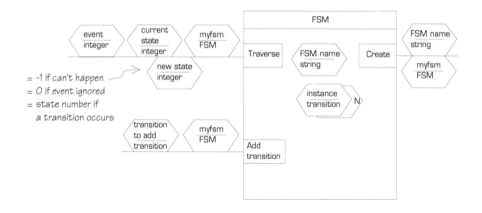

Figure 9.3.2: Class Diagram for the Finite State Model Class.

The FSM class, shown in Figure 9.3.2, serves to tie together all instances of Transition that compose a single state model. The exact physical data structure used for the instances of FSM and Transition will depend on the development environment (languages and class libraries) in use. We would expect a data structure similar to that shown in Figure 9.3.4. This might well be obtained by placing FSM as a child that inherits from a List class.

Active Instance, Figure 9.3.3, is an abstract class from which all instances that have state machines inherit their current state.

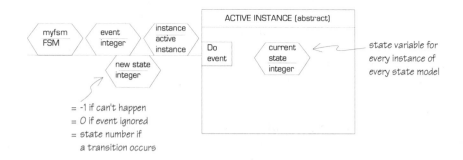

Figure 9.3.3: Class Diagram for the Active Instance Class.

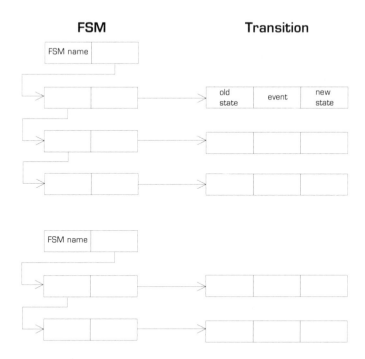

Figure 9.3.4: Data structures for the FSM and Transition classes.

Theory of Operation: Traversing a State Machine

When an application class receives an event (described in detail in Section 9.7), it invokes the operation Active Instance.Do Event, as shown in Figure 9.3.5. On this invocation, the application class passes as input parameters the event number that was received and handles for both the FSM to be traversed and for the instance that received the event, as shown in Figure 9.3.6. Do Event then picks up the current state of the active instance and invokes FSM.Traverse, passing as input parameters the current state, the received event, and the handle for the FSM to be traversed.

FSM.Traverse (Figure 9.3.7) now submits each transition of the specified FSM in turn to Transition.Match, until Transition.Match reports that a transition matching the event number and current state has been found (signified by the output parameter match having a value of true), and that the appropriate value for new state is known. FSM.Traverse now returns the new state to Active Instance.Do Event, which updates the state of the active instance and returns its value to the calling application class.

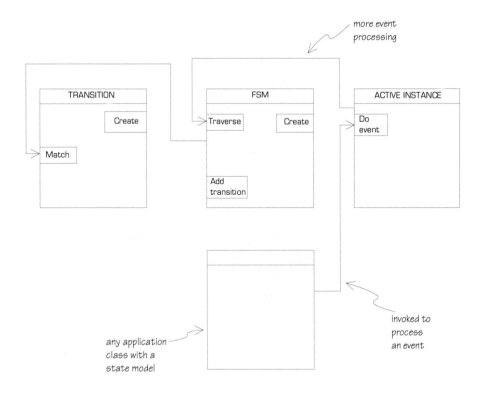

Figure 9.3.5: Dependencies associated with event processing.

If FSM.Traverse exhausts its list of transitions without getting a successful response from Transition.Match, we have encountered a "can't happen" cell from the state transition table. This indicates that an error has occurred, either in the analysis or in the implementation.

The appropriate way to handle the error depends to some extent on the nature of the application. At a minimum, we would expect FSM.Traverse to print a message indicating that an error has occurred. FSM.Traverse might then abort the program. Alternatively, it could return control to Active Instance.Do Event so that additional information (which instance of the state model failed) can be output for debugging purposes. Note that such output may be difficult to interpret: in many implementations the handle is only a pointer, so the programmers may not be able to determine which instance failed. A more polished solution places a deferring operation called Can't Happen Encoun-

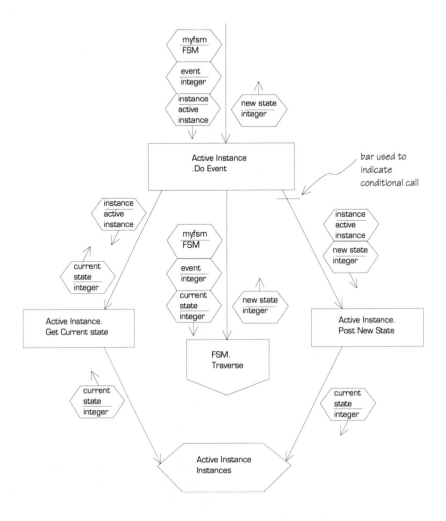

Figure 9.3.6: Class Structure Chart for the Active Instance class.

tered in Active Instance; Active Instance.Do Event could then do a polymorphic invocation of Can't Happen Encountered to transfer control to the application child class where clear text output can be supplied.

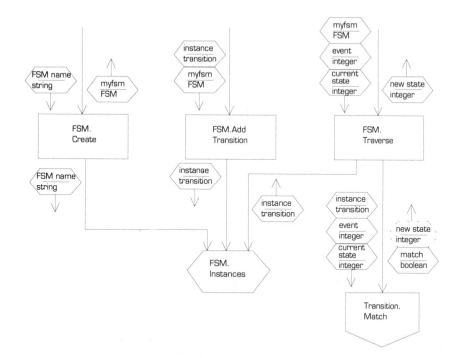

Figure 9.3.7: Class Structure Chart for the FSM class.

Theory of Operation: Initialization

Initialization of the state machine mechanism consists entirely of creating the appropriate instances of FSM and Transition. This is done by the application classes as described in Section 9.7. Three operations are provided for this purpose: FSM.Create, FSM.Add Transition, and Transition.Create.

The initialization begins when the application class calls FSM.Create (see Figure 9.3.8). FSM.Create accepts a text string name for the finite state model (to be used for printing "can't happen" messages) and returns a handle for the newly created instance of FSM.

After the application class has called FSM.Create, it then calls Transition.Create once for each cell (other than a can't happen cell) in its state transition table. Transition.Create creates the transition and calls FSM.Add Transition to link the transition into the FSM data structure. Transition.Create then returns control to the application class.

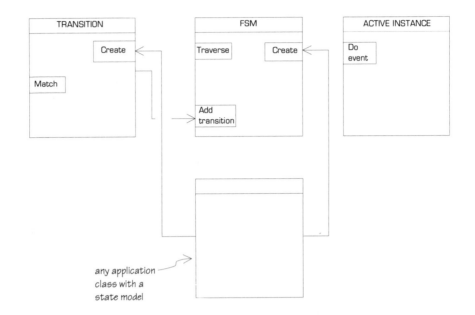

Figure 9.3.8: Dependencies associated with initialization of the state machine mechanism.

9.4 The Timer Class

The Timer class provides the mechanism to operate timers as defined in the OOA formalism. The class diagram for Timer is shown in Figure 9.4.1. Five published operations are defined for use by application classes:

Create	Creates a timer instance and returns its handle.
Delete	Deletes the specified instance.
Take Event TIM1	Sets the specified instance of timer to fire when the specified time interval has expired. When this timer fires, it will invoke a published operation (here, an "event taker") of some application class passing the handle of an instance of that application class.
Take Event TIM2	Resets the specified timer. Has no other effect.
Read Timer	Returns the time remaining on the specified timer. Has no other effect.

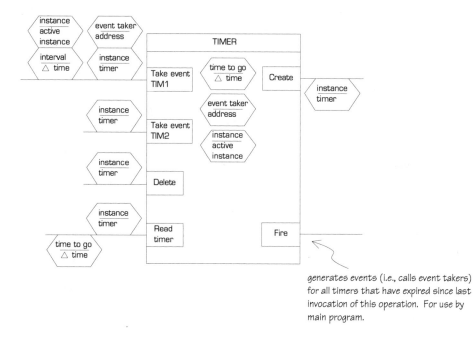

Figure 9.4.1: Class Diagram for the Timer Class.

The class operation, Fire, generates events (that is, invokes the specified event takers) associated with all timers that have expired since the previous invocation of Fire. This operation is provided for the use of the main program, as described in Section 9.8.

The Timer class can be implemented in a number of different ways, depending on the facilities available for keeping track of time. At a minimum, it requires access to a separate time-of-day clock or to an asynchronously counting clock.

9.5 Class Diagrams for the Application Classes

Patterns

Three different patterns are used to construct the application classes (see Figure 9.5.1).

171

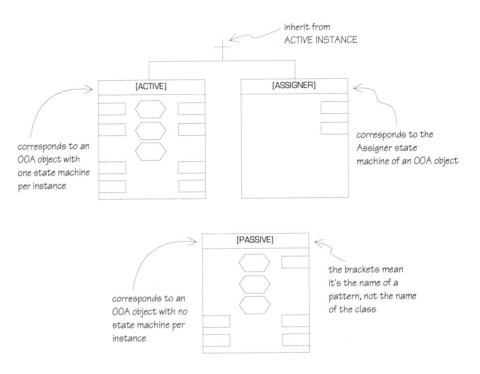

Figure 9.5.1: Types of Application Class.

- The *passive class* pattern is used to construct a class for an object that has no state model.

- The *active class* pattern is used to construct a class for an object that has one state machine for each instance.

- The *assigner* pattern is used to construct a class that corresponds to an Assigner state model in OOA.

In this section we present an orderly procedure for defining the external view of active, passive, and assigner classes in the form of class diagrams.

Passive Classes

An object that does not have a separate state machine for each instance is used to generate a passive class. The class diagram for a passive class is constructed by specifying:

- the class name
- instance components

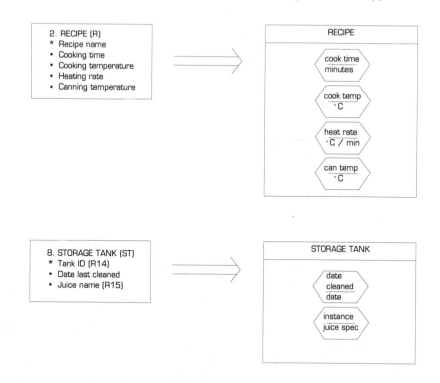

Figure 9.5.2: Constructing instance components for a class.

- accessors
- a constructor for pre-existing instances

Class name. The class name for a passive class is the same as that of the object from which it was generated.

Instance components. The first step in defining the published view of a class is to define the instance components for a typical unspecified instance of the class.

For each attribute of the object under consideration, define an instance component for the class being generated (Figure 9.5.2). The data type of each instance component is determined from the attribute's domain description.

There are two special cases that require further discussion.

  1. If an attribute is used only as an arbitrary identifier, the corresponding instance component is omitted. For example, the Recipe object in the

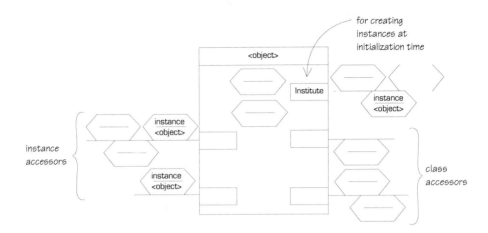

Figure 9.5.3: Pattern for the Class Diagram for a Passive Class.

juice plant has an arbitrary identifier which is used solely to distinguish one recipe from another. In object-oriented design, this purpose is served by the handle of the instance. Since the handle is not actually stored as part of the instance, no instance component corresponding to the identifier attribute appears on the class diagram.

Note, though, that some identifiers carry information that is needed in processing: Juice Specification.Juice Name is likely to be needed to print inventory reports. Such attributes are converted into instance components in the standard manner as described above.

2. Since the purpose of a referential attribute is to make a reference from one instance of an object to another, a referential attribute is converted into the handle of an instance of the related class. For example, the Storage Tank object in the juice plant example has a referential attribute Storage Tank.Juice Name that indicates which kind of juice is stored in the tank. This referential attribute is converted into a handle of an instance of Juice Specification as shown in Figure 9.5.2.

Accessors. Examine the object access model or the state process table to find all accessors assigned to the object under consideration. Define a published operation on the class diagram for each such accessor using an appropriate name for the published operation. In so doing, define the published operation as an instance operation if the accessor accesses the data of a single specified instance of the object; otherwise define the published operation as a class operation (Figure 9.5.3).

174

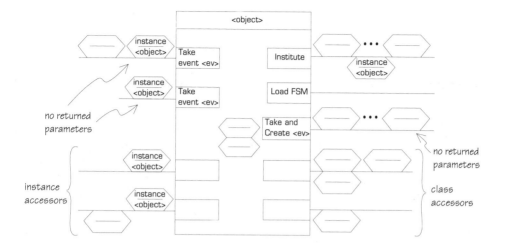

Figure 9.5.4: Pattern for the class diagram of an Active class.

Define the input and output parameters of the published operation to correspond with the input and output data elements shown on any ADFD that employs the accessor. The parameters should be named from the perspective of the class under construction.

Constructor for pre-existing instances. In most OOA models, it is assumed that instances of certain objects simply exist: no provision is made for their creation over the time scale covered by the analysis. For example, in the juice plant models, the objects Juice Specification, Recipe, Tank, and Pipe are cast as objects with previously-existing instances. If the object under consideration has this nature, provide a published class operation named Institute for constructing a pre-existing instance and returning its handle. This constructor will be invoked by the main module at initialization time.

Active Classes

An object that has a separate state machine for each instance is used to generate an active class. The class diagram (see Figure 9.5.4) for an active class is defined by specifying:

- the class name
- instance components
- accessors

- event takers
- an initializer
- a constructor for pre-existing instances

Class name. The class name for an active class is the same as that of the object from which it was generated.

Instance components. Instance components for an active class are defined in exactly the same way as are instance components for a passive class, except that no component is defined corresponding to the current state attribute. Instead, an instance of an active class inherits its current state component from the Active Instance class.

Accessors. Define a published operation for any accessor that (1) has been assigned to the object under consideration and (2) is used in an action of the state model of some other object. These accessors can be readily identified from the state process table. In so doing, remember to distinguish between instance and class operations, as was done when defining published operations for accessors in a passive class.

The input and output parameters of an accessor are defined in exactly the same manner as described for a passive class.

Event takers. Define a published operation corresponding to each event generator that is shown in the state process table as having been assigned to the object under consideration. Such published operations are known as *event takers*. There are two cases to consider:

1. If the event generated by the event generator does not cause a new instance of the object to be created, define the corresponding event taker as an instance operation. Name it Take Event <event label>.

2. If the event generated by the event generator causes a new instance of the object to be created, define the corresponding event taker as a class operation and name it Take and Create <event label>.

Define input parameters corresponding to each element of event data carried by the event. No output parameters are defined for an event taker, since an OOA event is an asynchronous communication which cannot therefore produce synchronous output.

The purpose of the event taker is, of course, to accept the event, determine what action (if any) should be executed, and to execute that action, thereby taking the instance into a new state.

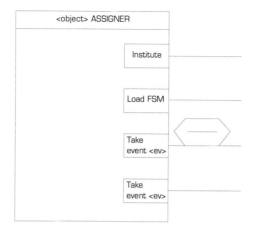

Figure 9.5.5: Pattern for the Class Diagram for an Assigner class.

Note that in this architecture we have defined the published interface of the class in terms of event takers, rather than the actions (or even processes that make up the action). This provides true semantic encapsulation of the state of an instance. Contrast this with a scheme in which the published interface is defined in terms of actions or processes. While such a scheme encapsulates the state of the instance in a legalistic sense, it induces a subtle coupling across the classes: in effect, it requires that a user of the class be sufficiently knowledgeable of the state model on which the class is based that the user can determine what action to call.

Initializer. Each active class must define a published class operation named Load FSM. This operation will be invoked by the main module at program initialization time to cause the active class to create its FSM, thereby enabling it to accept events.

Constructor for pre-existing instances. If the OOA models assume that instances of the object under consideration exist prior to the time scale of the analysis, provide a constructor to create an instance of the class in the same manner as for passive objects. The constructor is named Institute.

Assigner Classes

An Assigner state model is used to generate an assigner class. The assigner class so generated corresponds *only* to the state model: the object with which

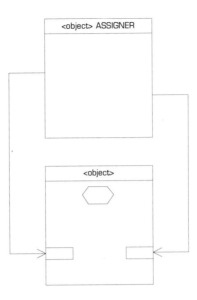

Figure 9.5.6: Possible dependencies between an <object> Assigner class and the corresponding active or passive <object> class.

the Assigner state model is associated is also used to generate either an active or a passive class (depending on whether it does or does not have a separate state machine for each instance of the object) and therefore any required instance components and accessors.

The class diagram for an assigner class (see Figure 9.5.5) is defined by specifying:

- the class name
- event takers
- an initializer
- a constructor

Note that the assigner class has no instance components (and therefore no accessors): the data describing each instance of the underlying object is encapsulated in the active (or passive) class generated from that object. As a result, the assigner class may need to invoke accessors of the active or passive class, as shown in Figure 9.5.6.

Class name. The class name for an assigner class is the same as that of the state model from which it is generated: <object> Assigner.

Event takers. Define an event taker for each event the Assigner state machine can receive. Since an event received by an assigner is not directed at a particular instance of an underlying object, no handle is provided as input to the event taker. Therefore, cast the event takers as class operations as shown in Figure 9.5.5.

Initializer. Define a published class operation Load FSM in exactly the same manner as for an active class.

Constructor. Provide a constructor named Institute. This operation will be invoked by the main module at initialization time to create the single instance of the assigner class. Note that this operation requires no input parameters.

9.6 Inheritance

Inheritance is used in this architecture for four purposes: to establish a data structure appropriate to the needs of each class, to implement the subtype-supertype construction of OOA, to incorporate classes of service domains, and, as discussed previously, to cause all classes based on state models to inherit their current state data from Active Instance.

Establishing Data Structure

The first step in designing the internals of a class is to decide on an appropriate data structure for storing the data describing each instance. The architecture does not specify how this is to be done, but leaves this matter up to the designer of each application class. Hence, if you have a class library containing implementation classes such as List, Stack, and Tree, we would suggest that you choose an appropriate class from this library to act as a parent to your application class. When making this selection, remember that if the application class has class operations that require traversal of all instances of the class, a linked structure will be required.

Subtype-Supertype

When subtype and supertype objects are used to generate classes in this architecture, define the class generated from the supertype object as a parent to the classes generated from the subtypes. Because OOA requires that any instance of a supertype have a corresponding instance of some subtype, the supertype class is necessarily an abstract class.

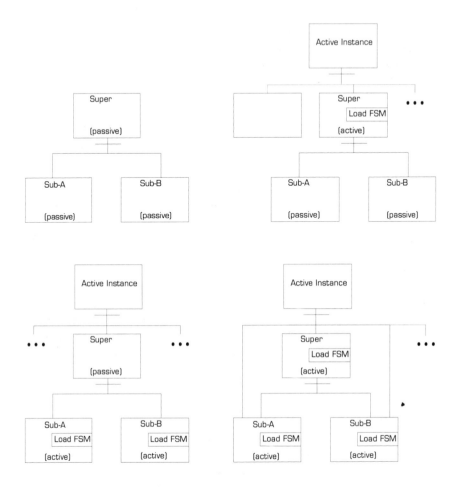

Figure 9.6.1: Inheritance relationships for subtype and supertype classes

If a subtype or supertype class has a state model, it must also inherit from Active Instance. The inheritance structure involving subtypes and supertypes can therefore take any of the four forms shown in Figure 9.6.1.

Service Domains

If instances of an application class need counterpart instances of a class from a service domain, an inheritance relationship can be established between the

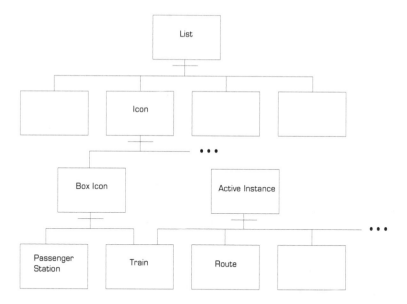

Figure 9.6.2: Inheritance structure used to establish counterparts with instances in a service domain.

class in the service domain (the parent) and the class in the application domain (the child). This can lead to a structure like that shown in Figure 9.6.2.

Note that on an inheritance diagram that includes classes from different domains, the most general classes — the implementation classes — will appear near the top of the diagram. Architectural and service classes appear in the middle, and the most specialized classes — the application classes — appear at the bottom. This is exactly the opposite of the domain chart, in which more specialized domains appear near the top and more general domains near the bottom.

9.7 Class Structure Charts for the Application Classes

The internal design of an application class is expressed in a class structure chart. Because the class structure chart can be quite large—larger than the page size of this book—we present the class structure charts of the application classes in a series of separated figures. Figure 9.7.1 gives a general impression

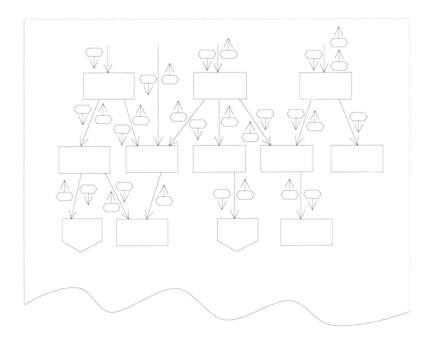

Figure 9.7.1: Shape of a completed class structure chart.

of what the completed class structure chart will look like when the detailed segments have been assembled.

Class Structure Chart for a Passive Class

The class structure chart for a passive class can be constructed almost mechanically from the class diagram. Place a module for each published operation (the accessors and the Institute operation) across the top of the chart. The input and output parameters for each operation can be copied from the class diagram. Connect the published operations with the instance data of the class, as shown in Figure 9.7.2.

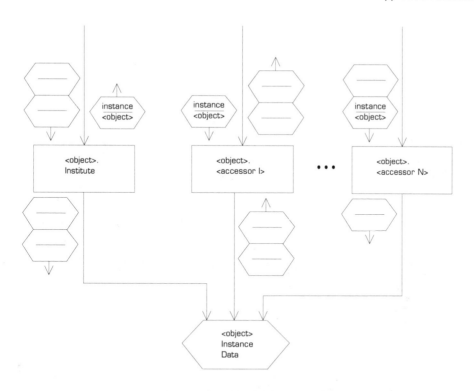

Figure 9.7.2: Pattern for the class structure chart of a passive class.

Class Structure Chart for an Active Class

An active class has a fairly elaborate class structure chart, which can be best described in four parts:

- initialization
- accessors
- event takers
- actions

Initialization. Two published operations are provided to initialize an active class: Institute and Load FSM. The portion of the class structure chart that depicts the initialization operations is shown in Figure 9.7.3. Note the use of class data: myfsm is a variable used to retain the handle of the FSM for the class. The transitions are also considered to be class data, since they apply equally to all instances of the class.

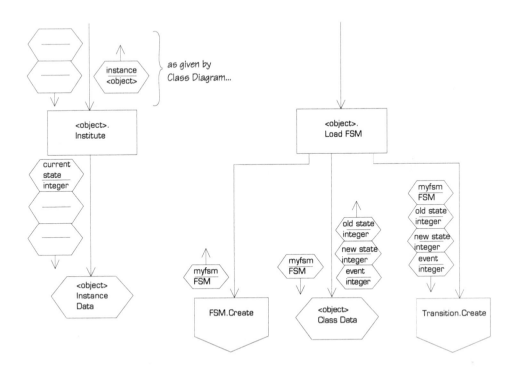

Figure 9.7.3: Pattern for the initialization section of the class structure chart for an active class.

Accessors. The portion of the class structure chart containing accessors for an active class is derived mechanically from the class diagram in exactly the same way as for a passive class.

Event takers. The portion of the class structure chart for a Take Event operation is shown in Figure 9.7.4. This operation finds the handle for the FSM belonging to the class and invokes Active Instance.Do Event to return the new state. It then executes the appropriate action as given by the new state. Remember that if the state number returned from Do Event is zero, no action is to be executed and if the state number is less than zero, a can't happen event has occurred.

A Take and Create operation causes a new instance to be created from the event data. Because this work is done in the action of the creation state, the take and create operation simply transfers control to the action of the creation state. The portion of the class structure chart for a Take and Create operation is shown in Figure 9.7.4.

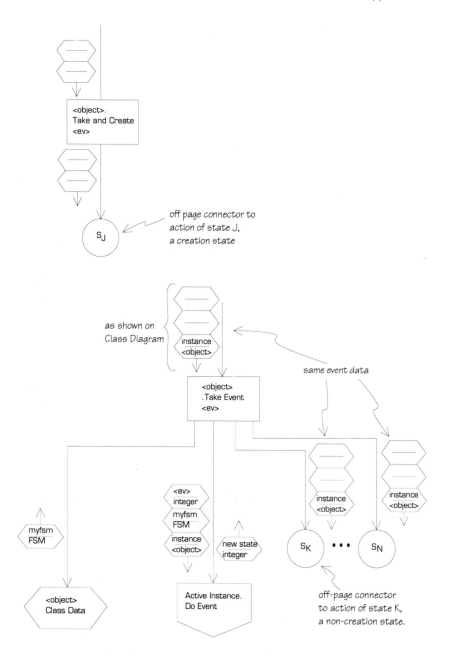

Figure 9.7.4: Patterns for the Take and Create and Take Event operations for an active class.

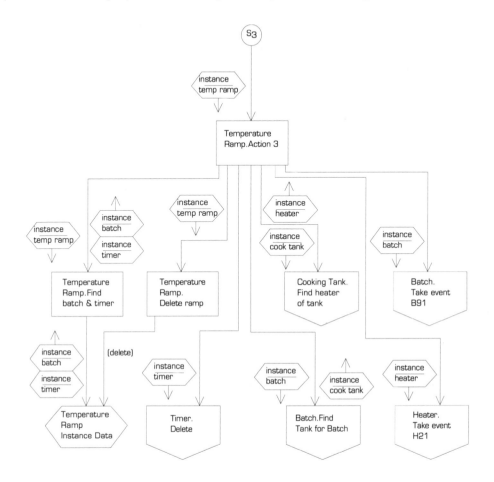

Figure 9.7.5: A portion of the class structure chart for the Temperature Ramp class. Compare this with the corresponding ADFD shown in Figure 6.2.6.

Actions. The portion of the class structure chart dealing with an action is constructed in a fairly mechanical manner from an ADFD. First create an unpublished operation named <object>.Action<k> where k is the state number with which the action is associated. This operation is called only from event takers in the same class, and is therefore not published.

The Action<k> operation, now seen as a module, receives as input all of the event data that was provided as input to the event taker. The module then proceeds to invoke modules corresponding to the accessors, tests, transforma-

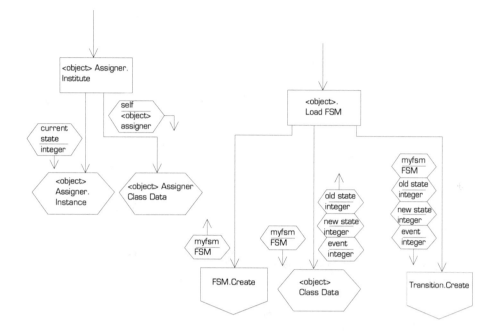

Figure 9.7.6: Pattern for the initialization section of the class
structure chart for an assigner class.

tions, and event generators shown on the ADFD. The purpose of the Action<k>
module is to invoke these separate modules in the required order, and to take
the output of one module and use it as input to the next. In this sense, the
Action<k> module acts as the wiring on the ADFD. This is easily seen by
comparing Figure 9.7.5 with the corresponding ADFD of Figure 6.2.6.

To construct the modules corresponding to processes on the ADFD, observe the
following conventions:

- If the process is an accessor assigned to another class, show it by means
  of the apron symbol. The accessor will have already been defined as a
  published operation on the class diagram of the other class.

- If the process is a published accessor assigned to this class, draw the
  invocation line from the Action<k> module to the accessor module on
  this class structure chart if the graphic layout permits. Otherwise,
  replicate the accessor module here in the action segment of the class
  structure chart, and annotate it to indicate that this is a published
  operation depicted elsewhere in the same class structure chart.

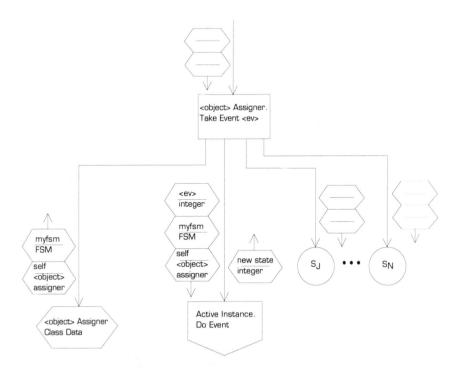

Figure 9.7.7: Pattern for a Take Event operation for an
assigner class.

- If the process is a test or transformation, the corresponding module is an unpublished operation of this class. Define the input and output parameters of the module to correspond with the data inputs and outputs shown on the ADFD.

- If the process is a test, define an additional output parameter that carries data telling the outcome of the test. This is a recasting of the control output of the ADFD in data. The Action<k> module will use the additional output parameter to determine which modules to call as the action is executed.

- If the process is an event generator, show an invocation of the corresponding published event taker, either in this or another class.

To maintain data consistency, cast the action so that all computation is complete before any event taker is invoked.

Class Structure Chart for an Assigner Class

The class structure chart of an assigner class is very similar to that of an active class. It is made up of three sections:

- initialization
- event takers
- actions

Initialization. The pattern for the initialization section of the class structure chart is shown in Figure 9.7.6. Note that the handle for the single instance of the class is retained as class data.

Event takers. The pattern for an event taker of an assigner class is given in Figure 9.7.7.

Actions. The actions for an assigner class are built according to the same rules as the actions for an active class.

9.8 The Main Program

The main program (Figure 9.8.1) is assigned three responsibilities in this architecture:

- invocation of the various initialization operations of the classes

- generation of the external events that initiate or continue a thread of control

- generation of timer events

Initialization

The first activity of the main program is to create any pre-existing instances of the application classes. If there are only a few such instances, this work can be coded directly in the main program in a straightforward manner as shown in Figure 9.8.1. There are, however, two possible complications. First, the number of pre-existing instances that need to be created may be large; in this case, we would suggest that the required information be prepared as data in a data file or database. The main program would then read and interpret the data to do the instance creation.

```
//
// Program to control the microwave oven
//
// Initialize all pre-existing instances.
//
     mytube := Power_tube::Institute ( )
     mylight := Light::Institute ( )
     myoven := Oven::Institute ( mytube, mylight )
//
// Load all FSMs
//
     Power_tube::Load FSM ( )
     Light::Load FSM ( )
     Oven::Load FSM ( )
//
// Now for the work
//
     do forever
        message_here := get_message ( message_buffer )
        if message_here then
           msg_type := unpack_message ( message_buffer )
           case of msg_type
              buttonpush:          myoven.Take_event_V1 ( )
                       end case
              dooropen: myoven.Take_event_V3 ( )
                       end case
              doorclosed:          myoven.Take_event_V4 ( )
                       end case
        endif
        Timer::Fire ( )  //     Fire outstanding timers, if any
     end forever
//
// End of microwave oven program
//
```

Figure 9.8.1: Structure of main program required by this architecture. The language is a pseudocode loosely based on C++.

The second complication has to do with the order in which the instances are created. In a number of cases, you will find that you need the handle of one instance (call it instance B) in order to create another instance (instance A). For example, in Figure 9.5.2, you cannot create an instance of Storage Tank until you have the handle of the required instance of Juice Specification.

The main module must also invoke the Load FSM operation of all active and assigner classes. This can be done either before or after creating the pre-existing instances.

190

External Events

Once the classes have been initialized, the real work can begin. In the simplest case, the main program controls the activity of the classes by executing a single pre-planned scenario: a sequence of calls to the event takers of the various classes. Each call corresponds to the generation of some external event along the thread of control.

In a more complex case, the main program receives messages from other tasks to determine which of several external events to generate. This case is shown in Figure 9.8.1, in which three messages corresponding to different external events are handled.* Note that the main program acts as a mediator between the classes and elements outside this program: here, some PIO or user interface code that converts interrupts into messages.

Flow of Control

When a message is received by the main program and an event taker is invoked, control does not necessarily return immediately to the main loop. The action invoked as a result of calling the event taker may itself invoke other event takers, which may, in turn, invoke still others. Eventually, control will be given to an action that generates no events; at this point control will return from the action to the event taker that invoked it and then to the previous action that invoked the event taker. This pattern will continue back up the calling hierarchy until control eventually returns to the main loop.**

Timers

The main program is also responsible for calling Timer.Fire sufficiently often that events corresponding to the expiration of a timer can be generated in a timely fashion. The program in Figure 9.8.1 has been constructed to support this responsibility: Timer.Fire is called on every pass through the loop. In addition, all operations called from within the loop return control fairly promptly on the time scale on which a timer operates:

---

*These are the same external events shown on the object communication model of Figure 5.1.1.
**Since OOA permits generation of the same event multiple times along the same thread of control, this architecture (as well as any other fully synchronous architecture) requires re-entrancy at some point in the implementation. In this architecture, the event takers and <object>.Action<k> modules must be re-entrant.

- Because the time rules regulating the construction of an action require that each action run to completion without external intervention, we are assured that the chain of execution emanating from an event taker proceeds to completion at computational speed.

- The get_message operation returns control almost immediately whether or not a message is available to be received.

9.9 Extending and Using the Architecture

Variations

There are a number of minor variations you might want to consider when producing an architecture similar to the one described in the chapter.

FSM and Transition. Some improvement in performance can be obtained by merging the FSM and Transition classes. We chose to keep them separate in this presentation only for ease of explanation.

Assigners and associated passive classes. The <object> Assigner and passive <object> application classes can be merged. If this is done, some accessors of the encapsulated data may not need to be published.

Constructors. In certain cases, the rules given here lead to the definition of both an Institute operation and a separate create accessor. If both operations have the same input parameters (which is likely), then the operations are the same and should be accomplished by the same module. If your implementation language allows, we would suggest that this module be named both Institute and the natural OOA name of the accessor, in order to preserve uniformity of the interfaces on the class diagrams.

Work Products

Traditional approaches to design make the assumption that the designer will produce a separate graphic model for each program and class in the finished system. However, when taking a transformational approach as in Recursive Design, the design is so uniform that production of complete class structure charts (for example) would be a lengthy clerical task of limited value.

Instead we suggest that you produce class diagrams and class structure charts in detail only as archetype diagrams — diagrams that indicate where specialization must be accomplished by name substitution. These diagrams, together with the rules for making the name substitutions, amount to a specification of the architecture.

Once having done this, produce

- the class diagram for each class in the application domain
- the action segments of the class structure charts.*

The remainder of the design can be expressed in code templates: pieces of code containing placeholders where appropriate names need to be substituted. See Figure 9.9.1 for an example.

Such a strategy opens up the possibility of automatically generating code tailored exactly to the architecture chosen for a particular project. We have seen this strategy demonstrated with different degrees of automation on several client projects and find it very promising. Consider the implications of this comment:

> "We found an incompatibility between our architecture and the user interface package we needed to use. The problem impacted dozens of classes; resolving it required several delicate modifications be made to all the classes affected. Since we were able to make the required changes in the templates, when we regenerated and recompiled the code — an all-day project — we knew the modifications had been made accurately every-where. I hesitate to think how many weeks this problem would have cost us had we taken the 'every class handcrafted with loving care' approach."

Multitasking

The architecture described in this chapter assumes that each task is surrounded by a "visibility boundary" such that one task cannot directly access code within another task. If this assumption holds in your development environment — you are using C++ on Unix or VMS, for example — you will find it a non-trivial design job to extend this architecture to support more than the token multitasking supplied here. The fundamental problem has to do with achieving access to the data of an instance in another task without violating the time rules. The last

---

*Note that if you have produced your OOA models with a CASE tool, most of the information required to generate these diagrams has already been entered in the database underlying the tool. If the program allows read access to that database, you can probably produce specialized reports to aid in the generation of the diagrams.

```
//      Template for the interface to an active class using C++
//
//
//      Angle brackets indicate a name to be replaced by the template processor.
//      The template processor may be a programmer, an editor, a special purpose
//      program linked to a CASE tool, or a preprocessor.
//
//      An attribute grammar may be used to specify the replacement rules precisely.
//
//      <active class name> and <active class type> are the name and type of the
//      active class being defined.
//
//      Subscripted variables are used to indicate the ith element as follows:
//          attr_i is the ith declared attribute of the source object
//          attr_i type is the type of the ith attribute, derived from its domain description
//          event_i is an event number handled by the class for Take Event and Take and Create
//          dataset_i is the event data for the ith event
//          dataset_i attr_j is the jth attribute of the ith dataset
//
//      Declare the class

class <active class name> : public active_instance {

//      Declare the instance components

private:

        <attr_1 type> <attr_1>;
        <attr_2 type> <attr_2>;
        <attr_3 type> <attr_3>;
        <attr_4 type> <attr_4>;
          . . .

public:

//      First, the class operations

//      <active class type> Institute( <attr_1 type>, <attr_2 type>, . . . ) is written as:
        <active class name> ( <attr_1 type>, <attr_2 type>, . . . );
        void Load_FSM();

//      Now the class-based event takers

        void Take_and_Create_<event_1>( <dataset_1 attr_1 type>, <dataset_1 attr_2 type>, . . . );
        void Take_and_Create_<event_2>( <dataset_2 attr_1 type>, <dataset_2 attr_2 type>, . . . );
          . . .

//      Now the instance operations, event takers first

        void Take_Event_<event_1>( <dataset_1 attr_1 type>, <dataset_1 attr_2 type>, . . . );
        void Take_Event_<event_2>( <dataset_2 attr_1 type>, <dataset_2 attr_2 type>, . . . );

//      Now the read accessors, conventionally called Read_<attr_i>

        <attr_1 type> Read_<attr_1>();
        <attr_2 type> Read_<attr_2>();
        <attr_3 type> Read_<attr_3>();
          . . .

}
```

Figure 9.9.1: C++ template for the interface of an active class.

point is key: We have explored the properties of some architectures that do not preserve the time rules and have determined that in such cases the design itself may induce a deadlock that was not present in the original OOA models. Note that concurrency and instance sharing are receiving (1990, 1991) significant attention as research topics [2, 3]. We expect it may take some time before widely-applicable techniques for dealing with these issues become well-understood.

Finally, should you be working in an environment where the task boundary does not coincide with a visibility boundary (as in Ada), we would suggest that you consider the architecture described in [4] as a starting point.

9.10 Recursive Design

Let us recapitulate what we have done in this chapter, now from the point of view of the method (Recursive Design) rather than the result (a particular object-oriented design).

Structural Elements and Rules of the Architecture

First, we defined the conceptual entities of the architecture: the four special architectural classes, the application classes, accessors, event takers and the like. These entities provide the structural elements of the architecture.

We also defined structural rules: required relationships between the various structural elements. For example

A passive class has published accessors but no event takers.

An assigner class has class operations only: an Institute operation, a Load FSM operation, and event takers.

Because we had a notation appropriate for depicting a design based on classes, we expressed the structural rules in an archetype form of that notation: the patterns for class diagrams and class structure charts for the application classes.

Alternatively, the structural elements and rules could have been defined in terms of OOA. Figure 9.10.1 provides an information model of the architecture wherein the structural elements appear as objects and the structural rules are expressed as relationships.

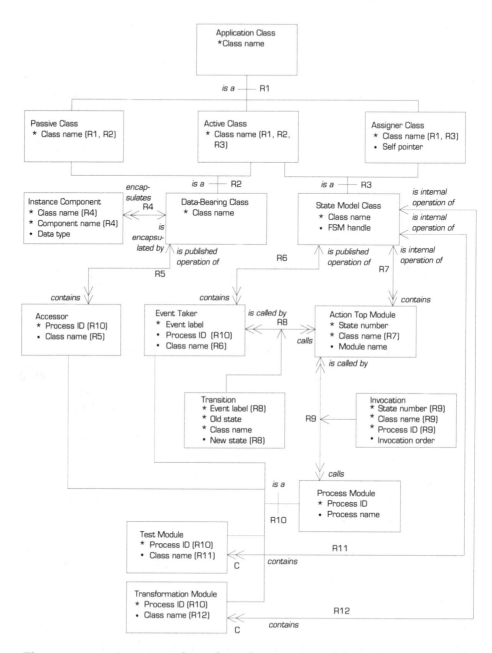

Figure 9.10.1: An extract from the information model for the synchronous object-oriented architecture. Those portions of the model that deal with initialization and with the input and output parameters of the processes have been omitted for lack of space.

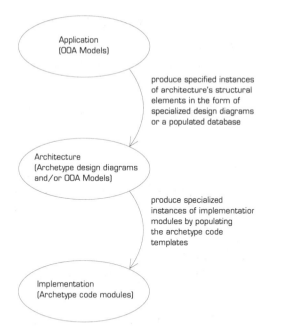

Figure 9.10.2: Transforming the application models into an implementation.

Transformation Rules: Application to Architecture

Once the conceptual entities of the architecture were defined, we prescribed how to transform elements of the application domain (attributes, events, processes and so on) into specified instances of the architectural objects (see Figure 9.10.2).

These transformation rules were described as a procedure for producing specified instances of the architectural objects (a Batch class, a Temperature Ramp class and so on) in the form of specialized class diagrams and class structure charts — specializations of the archetype class diagrams and class structure charts.

Alternatively, the procedure could have been based on the information model for the architecture. If you were to make a database with a schema corresponding to the information model of the architecture, the transformation rules would explain how to create the specified instances of the architectural objects by populating the database.

Transformation Rules: Architecture to Implementation

In the final step we transformed the architectural domain into the implementation domain. To do this, we expressed the modules of the archetype class structure charts as archetype code (code templates) in the chosen implementation language. The templates can then be filled out either from the populated architecture database or from the specialized class structure charts.

References

[1] Sally Shlaer and Stephen J. Mellor, "Recursive Design," in *Computer Language*, Vol. 7, No. 3, Miller-Freeman Publications, San Francisco, March 1990.

[2] *Proceedings of the Conference on Object-Oriented Programming: Systems, Languages, and Applications (OOPSLA/ECOOP '90)*, Addison-Wesley, Reading, Mass., 1990.

[3] David Jordan, "Instantiation of C++ Objects in Shared Memory," *Journal of Object-Oriented Programming*, Vol. 4, No. 1, SIGS Publications, New York, March-April 1991.

[4] Rick Hill, "Object-Oriented Design in Ada: A Transformational Approach Based on Object-Oriented Analysis," in *Proceedings of the Structured Development Forum (SDF-XI)*, Structured Development Forum, San Diego, April 1990.

Appendices

OODLE:
A Language-Independent
Notation for
Object-Oriented Design

This paper presents a language-independent graphical notation for depicting the design of an object-oriented program, library, or environment. Four distinct diagrams are prescribed. Each diagram is designed for specific uses and identified users. The diagrams are interrelated by a layering scheme to provide a basis for document organization as well as for navigation or browsing in an automated system.

The notation has been named OODLE, an acronym for Object-Oriented Design LanguagE.

1 Goals

1.1 What to Represent

In developing the OODLE notation, we laid out the following goals with respect to what the notation should and should not seek to represent:

- The notation must represent the fundamental concepts of OOD (including encapsulation of data, inheritance, and polymorphism) in an intuitive manner.

- Data typing should be strongly emphasized and represented. Experienced designers take careful account of data types, regardless of the level of support for typing in the intended implementation language.

- The design notation should not seek to represent all possible constructs (and combinations of constructs) of a programming language or languages. It should concentrate on fundamental language-independent concepts such as visibility of operations, partitioning of code, invocation and exceptions. At the same time, the notation should be rich enough to support key design decisions that need to be accounted for to render the design into an implementation language.

- The notation should be susceptible to language-specific interpretations.

1.2 Style of Representation

During development of this notation, we investigated numerous other design notations—object-oriented and otherwise—to assess their strengths and limitations under practical circumstances. In this process we identified some notational properties and strategies that contributed to (or detracted from) the usefulness of a notation in a significant way. The result of this work is summarized in the following goals related to style of representation.

Hand-drawable

Despite the popularity of CASE tools, much initial design work is carried out at the whiteboard or around the conference table. The notation should therefore be usable by a designer working in such a situation. This "hand-drawable" requirement led us to reject representations that depend upon shading, discrimination between different line widths, and symbols that are too fine to be drawn with a marker on a whiteboard.

No Needless Differences

The notation should not be needlessly different from notations presently published or supported by common CASE tools. The purposes of this goal are these: First, to make it easier for a practitioner to learn the notation; second, to facilitate enhancement of existing CASE tools to support the notation; and third, to encourage creative exploitation of existing tools not originally intended to support OOD [5].

Single vs. Multiple Views

The notation should not seek to represent every aspect of the design on a single diagram. We have experienced two practical problems with such single-view notations: First, a large and complex repertoire of symbols is required to differentiate between the different constructs being represented [6]. This property conflicts with the goals of being easy to learn and easy to draw by hand.

Secondly, notations based on a single view of the design are unlikely to represent all aspects of the design equally well. For example, while the Ada structure graph notation [2] is extremely successful in representing visibility relationships between design components, it is less effective in depicting the flow of control.

Density of Information

Each view should contain enough information to make it worth producing, but not so much as to make it unmanageable or unreadable.

Consistency Rules

In a multi-view notation, rules are required so that a designer (as well as an automated system) can determine if the different views of the design are consistent with one another. The notation should be defined in such a way that consistency rules can be stated with precision.

Inclusion Rules

In order to make some notations workable, the designer must select — on a case-by-case basis — which design components he or she wishes to represent, and suppress representation of other components [7]. Notations of this sort have a degree of ambiguity: If a component is missing, the reader cannot tell whether it has been omitted for clarity of representation or whether the designer has designed it out. The notation should therefore be accompanied by rules that state precisely what design components are to be represented (or not represented) on any view.

No Delicate Placement Requirements

Some notations require the designer to place symbols or labels very carefully on the diagram in order to capture the intended associations. For example, structure charts [4, 8] require that data couple symbols be associated with connector lines, and that names or labels be attached to the data couple symbols. On even a moderately small diagram, it can be difficult to place the couples and labels so that the couples, labels, and connectors are all associated unambiguously.

The notation should reduce such delicate placement requirements to the greatest extent possible.

Alternative Representations

The notation should allow for some alternative representations. Our experience with the notation for OOA has convinced us that some flexibility on this matter is desirable so that projects can establish representation conventions most easily supported by their CASE tools.

2. Components of the Notation

The following diagrams have been developed to depict four significant aspects of the design:

Class diagram. A class diagram depicts the external view of a single class. This diagram is based on notations of Booch [1] and Buhr [2], but shows considerably more detail of the external specification.

Class structure chart. The class structure chart is used to show the internal structure of the code of the operations of the class. This chart is based on traditional structure charts [4, 8], enhanced to show additional concepts pertinent to object-oriented development.

Dependency diagram. The dependency diagram depicts the client-server (invocation) and friend relationships that hold between the classes.

Inheritance diagram. The inheritance diagram shows the inheritance relationships that pertain between the classes. This diagram is derived from the information modeling notation of OOA.

The relationships between these four graphic representations is shown in the sketch in Figure 2.1.1.

The remainder of this paper describes the diagrams in detail. In the descriptions, we use *published operation* to mean a method or function that is made generally available for use from outside a class. The traditional term *invocation* is used to indicate a synchronous transfer of control from one function or

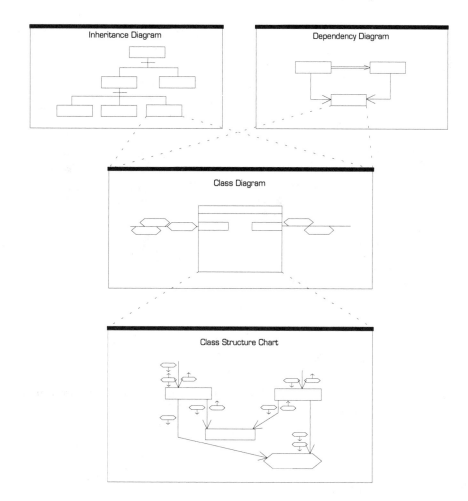

Figure 2.1.1: Relationships between the OODLE Diagrams.

procedure to another. We prefer this term because the object-oriented *send a message* is subject to misinterpretation by real-time software engineers.

Class is used in the sense of C++ and Smalltalk. *Instance* means a single occurrence of the data structure on which the class is based. Finally, we use the term *utility function* to indicate a unit of code (such as Allocate Memory or Copy String) that does not belong to any class and does not reference any operation of a class.

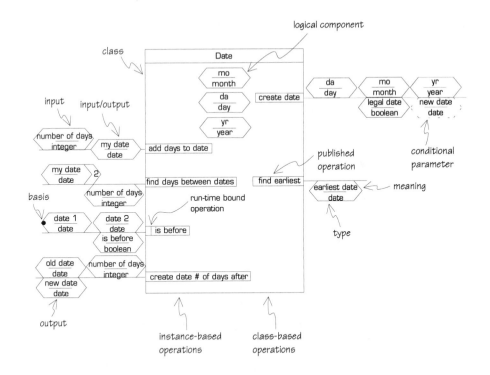

Figure 3.2.1: Class Diagram. This figure illustrates the most commonly used elements of the notation.

3. Class Diagram

3.1 Purpose

The class diagram depicts the external view of a single class. One class diagram is prepared for each class in the design.

The engineer who wishes to invoke operations of a previously-developed class can find all the information he or she requires on the class diagram; in this situation, class diagrams act as a programmer's reference manual. In addition, the class diagram provides an external or interface specification to the engineer responsible for designing the internal structure of the class.

3.2 Symbology

Class

The class being represented on the class diagram is shown as a square or rectangle labeled with the name of the class, as shown in Figure 3.2.1. This graphical element is referred to as the *class box*. If the class is an abstract class (*deferred class* in Eiffel [3]), annotate the class box as shown in Figure 3.2.2.

Logical Components

In OOD, each class is designed around a data type appropriate for storing information about an instance of that class. The logical components of the data type are represented on the class diagram by small divided hexagons (known as *woks*) within the class box. Each such logical component is labeled with the meaning (in the upper half of the wok) and type (in the lower half) of the component. The placement of the woks inside the class box is intended as a visual reminder that the elements of the data structure are not directly accessible from outside the class.

Note that a logical component appearing on the class diagram does not necessarily imply that the implemented data structure will contain that component as a separate data element. For example, in the class shown in Figure 3.2.1, it is quite likely that the data structure as implemented will contain only a single data element (day number since some absolute starting date). Nonetheless, from an external perspective, these three logical components can be distinguished.

Published Operations

Published operations are provided to access and manipulate the logical components of the data type. The published operations are represented by rectangles inside but adjacent to the boundary of the class box. Each published operation is labeled with a meaningful name.

The published operations of a class can be divided into two categories:

Instance-based operations. An instance-based operation is one in which the caller of the operation supplies an instance of the underlying data structure (typically in the form of a pointer). The operation then manipulates that data structure. Published operations in this category are placed on the left side of the class box.

Class-based operations. Operations for which the caller does not supply a particular instance of the underlying data structure are known as *class-based*. Class-based operations include queries, iterators, and create operations. Class-based operations are placed on the right side of the class box.

The notation distinguishes between instance-based and class-based operations for two reasons:

1. The design of the data structure used to store information about an instance can be strongly affected by the need to support class operations. The class operations have therefore been grouped together to assist the engineer designing the internals of the class using the class diagram as an external specification.

2. In Smalltalk, the class- and instance-based operations form separate inheritance hierarchies. Because the class diagram is used as the basis of the inheritance diagram (see Section 7), the instance- vs. class-based distinction is stated on the class diagram.

Parameters

Inputs and outputs of each operation are shown as woks attached to a *parameter line* extending from the operation outside the class box. Input parameters are shown above the parameter line, while output parameters are shown below the line. Inputs that are returned to the caller with a modified value are shown on the parameter line. When a parameter representing an instance is shown on the parameter line, the interpretation is that the instance pointer has been modified.

If a parameter is passed or returned only under certain circumstances (that is, it is a conditional parameter), the wok is depicted in dotted lines.

If several parameters of the same meaning and type are input to (or output by) the operation, the diagram can be condensed by use of the *replicate* notation illustrated by the woks of the Find Days Between Dates operation shown in Figure 3.2.1. Here the number 2 indicates that exactly two date parameters are being supplied to the operation.

Note that the parameters here are formal parameters; as a result the "meaning" given in the upper half of the wok is a name for the formal parameter selected so as to be meaningful to the user of the class.

Basis and Ordering of Woks

When the class diagram is used as graphical documentation for users of existing classes, the programmer may need explicit information to allow him or her to determine which parameter is considered to be the basis of the instance operation. The *basis marker* shown on an input parameter to the Is Before operation of Figure 3.2.1 is available for this purpose.

Similarly, the programmer needs to know in what order to supply the parameters to invoke the published operation. This need can be met by establishing a language-dependent convention for the ordering of woks on the parameter line.

Deferment

In order to make effective use of polymorphism, the designer of an object-oriented environment may wish to impose a degree of uniformity on the design of classes by a strategy called *deferment*. Using this strategy, the designer will specify, in some class, the name of an operation and the input/output parameters the operation requires. The operation — known as the *deferring* operation — is not implemented in this class. Instead, a *deferred* operation is supplied in classes that inherit from the class in which the deferring operation was specified. The deferred operations must all have the same name and input/output parameters as the deferring operation. This strategy is supported in Eiffel, where the operations are known as *deferred routines*; in other languages, the strategy may be supportable only by convention.

If a published operation is a deferring operation, the box containing the name of the operation is drawn with dotted lines (Figure 3.2.2). The deferred operations that are defined in conformance with the deferring operation appear on other class diagrams using the normal notation of any published operation.

Compile-time vs. Run-time Binding

In OOD, it is common to define published operations of the same name in several different classes. In such a situation the selection of exactly which operation to invoke varies in a language-dependent manner. In Smalltalk, the selection is determined at run time and is based on the dynamic type of the instance: the class in which the instance was created. By contrast, in Ada this determination is made at compile time and is based on the static (declared) type of the instance. A more complex situation exists in C++, in which both possibilities are supported.

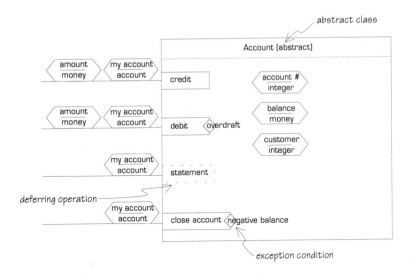

Figure 3.2.2: Class Diagram illustrating the representation of abstract classes, exception conditions, and deferring operations.

To distinguish between an operation that is bound at compile time, and an operation that is bound at run time (virtual function in C++), mark the outer edge of the operation box with a double bar if it is bound at run time. This notation is illustrated in Figure 6.2.1 (of this appendix) by the published operations Regular Checking Account.Debit Service Charge and Checking with Interest Account.Debit Service Charge.

Exceptions

If a published operation can raise one or more exceptions that the caller is expected to handle, show each exception condition in a separate diamond on the inner boundary of the operation, as illustrated in Figure 3.2.2. This compact representation was borrowed from OOSD [6].

3.3 Alternative Representations

As an alternative to a dotted wok, one can annotate the wok with the letter "c" to indicate that the parameter is a conditional one. This is analogous to the OOA representation of conditional relationship.

For hand-drawn diagrams, a "clamshell" (a small oval divided by a horizontal line) makes a good substitute for a wok.

4. Class Structure Chart

4.1 Purpose

The class structure chart is used to show the structure of the code as well as the flow of data and control within the class. A separate class structure chart is produced for each class. The diagram is intended as a design tool for the engineer responsible for designing the internals of a particular class.

4.2 Symbology

The class structure chart, like the traditional structure chart, is based on the concept of a module: a piece of code that is invoked and, when complete, returns control to the caller. Each module is represented by a rectangle (or apron, as described below) on the class structure chart, as illustrated in Figure 4.2.1.

Invocation

A module may invoke one or more other modules. An invocation is depicted on the class structure chart by an arrow from the calling module to the called module. Any data passed to or returned by the called module is represented by a wok labeled with meaning and type, consistent with the symbology of the class diagram. An arrow attached to the wok tells the direction of flow of the data. If input data is modified and then returned to the caller, the wok carrying that data will have two arrows attached: one showing the input direction, and one the output direction. If the input (or output) is produced only under certain circumstances, the wok is drawn with a dotted border.

Module Names

Each module appearing on the class structure chart is labeled with a name. If a module is part of a class, it is labeled as

      class name.module name.

If a module is not part of any class, it is labeled with a distinctive module name only: Allocate Memory (see Figure 4.2.1) is an example of such a module.

Primary Modules

A *primary module* represents the unit of code that receives control when a published operation is invoked. There is one primary module for each non-deferring published operation defined on the class diagram. The primary modules appear near the top of the class structure chart. Graphically, the distinctive feature of a primary module is that the class structure chart shows it being invoked, but does not depict or identify the external caller. If, in addition, a primary module is invoked by a module within this class, the internal invocation will be shown in the standard manner.

Note that the names appearing on the primary modules correspond exactly to the names of the class and published operations on the class diagram.

Inputs and outputs of a primary module must agree exactly in meaning, number, and type with the external woks shown with the corresponding published operation on the class diagram.

Foreign Modules

A *foreign module* on a class structure chart is a module that does not belong to the class being depicted. A foreign module may be either a module of another class, a utility function, or a friend function that is not a member of any class. A foreign module is represented by an apron symbol, as illustrated by the Allocate Memory module shown in Figure 4.2.1.

The apron symbol was chosen to represent a foreign module because of its resemblance to the commonly-used off-page connector. This is intended as a visual reminder that any chain of invocation that continues below the foreign module is documented elsewhere — in the class structure chart for another class or, in the case of a utility function, in traditional structure charts used to document a conventional library.

When the foreign module is a published operation of another class, the inputs and outputs of the module must match in type (but not necessarily in meaning) with the formal parameters shown on the class diagram that defines the published operation. This point is illustrated in Figures 3.2.2 and 4.2.3: In Figure 3.2.2, the Account.Debit operation requires a formal parameter of meaning "amount" and type "money." In one invocation of Account.Debit on Figure 4.2.3, the corresponding input parameter is of also type "money", but the meaning is "service charge." This is consistent with rules for traditional structure charts, in which the data couples are named from the perspective of the invoking module.

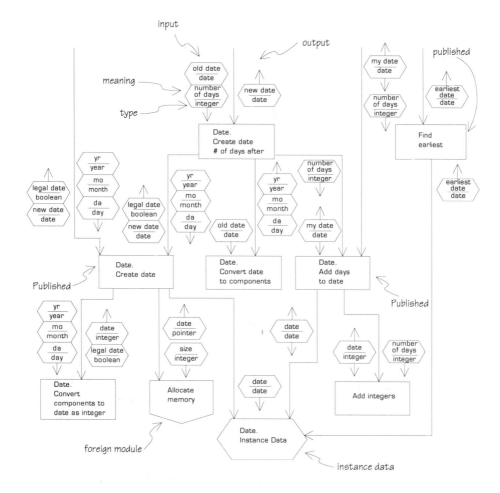

Figure 4.2.1: Class Structure Chart for the Date class. This Class Structure Chart corresponds to the Class Diagram of Figure 3.2.1. Not all operations from the Class Diagram are shown.

Instance Data

The instance data of a class is represented by the large hexagon symbol commonly used to represent a *shared data area* or *data-only module.* The hexagon is labeled as

Class Name.Instance Data

as shown in Figure 4.2.1 (Date.Instance Data).

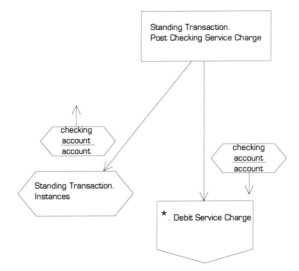

Figure 4.2.2: Polymorphism. The class of the Debit Service Charge operation will be determined at run time.

If the class contains a module that directly accesses instance data of another class ("is a friend of"), the instance data of the other class will *also* appear as a hexagon on the class structure chart. That is, a class structure chart may show multiple instance data hexagons, which are distinguishable from one another by the class names with which they are labeled.

When a module accesses instance data, a connector is drawn from the module to the appropriate instance hexagon. The data elements that are read or written by the module are shown by woks with arrows attached to indicate the direction of data flow.

Other Persistent Data

The hexagon symbol can also be used to represent other persistent data required by the class. When used for such a purpose, label the hexagon with a distinctive name prefixed by the name of the class:

Class Name.Class Data

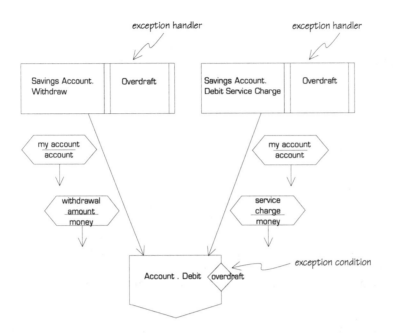

Figure 4.2.3: Exceptions. The exception condition overdraft is raised in Account.Debit. Two exception handlers are provided: Savings Account.Withdraw.Overdraft and Savings Account.Debit Service Charge.Overdraft.

Polymorphism

At design time, a polymorphic invocation is an invocation of one of a set of instance-based published operations, where all of the published operations in the set have the same module name but differing class names. When indicating a polymorphic invocation, the designer is stating that (1) the published operation to be invoked will be selected at run time, and (2) the selection will be based on the type of the instance.

Polymorphic invocation is represented on the class structure chart as invocation of a foreign module whose name is *.module name. This notation is illustrated in Figure 4.2.2.

Exceptions

If a module can raise one or more exception conditions, show the name of each exception in a diamond on the side of the rectangle (or apron) representing the module.

If an exception handler is provided as part of a module, show the exception handler as an additional rectangle appended to the right of the rectangle representing the module. Figure 4.2.3 provides an example of the notation for exceptions. Note that the sides of the rectangles representing exception handlers have been drawn in double lines.

4.3 Discussion

The wok notation arose in response to the "delicate placement problem" discussed previously. We believe it is reasonably successful, in that it binds three of the required components (meaning, type, and direction of flow) together in a single visual element. The fourth component — the invocation connector — can also be bound by requiring that the wok actually touch the connector. This last part of the solution still constitutes a delicate placement problem when drawings are made by hand; presumably an automated tool could assist in the precise placement.

As an alternative to the wok notation, one can use the standard data couples of structured design. The couples then should be annotated with both meaning and type.

To depict the internal design of the main program in a manner compatible with the class structure chart, we would suggest that one use standard structure chart notation, substituting woks for the data couples, and apron symbols for invocation of published operations of the classes.

5. Dependency Diagram

5.1 Dependency

Dependency is the object-oriented analog of coupling in structured design. In general terms, the greater the dependency between classes, the more problems are likely to arise during maintenance: With a high degree of dependency, modifications made to one class are likely to require that corresponding modifications be made to the code of the other class.

We distinguish between two types of dependency: client-server and friends.

Client-Server

When a module of one class (call it Class A) invokes a published operation of another class (Class B), a client-server relationship is said to exist between the classes. The invoking class (Class A) is considered to be the client, while the invoked class is considered to be the server.

A client-server relationship results in a low degree of dependency between the classes concerned, since the interactions are localized to the published operations on the encapsulation boundary of the server.

Friends

For reasons of performance or reduction of complexity, the designer may choose to allow certain violations of the encapsulation boundary. Some object-oriented languages provide facilities to support intended violations in a controlled manner. The intended violations give rise to the friend relationship.

When a module of one class (Class A) either (1) invokes an internal operation of another class (Class B) or (2) makes direct access of the data of the other class, Class A is said to be a friend of Class B.

Similarly, when a module that is not a part of any class either invokes an internal operation of some class or makes direct access to the data of the class, the module is said to be a friend of the class. Such a module is called a friend module.

A friend relationship indicates a high degree of dependency between the participating components.

Purpose of the Diagram

The dependency diagram depicts all of the dependency relationships that pertain between classes and non-class friend modules. This diagram provides a road-map to the program (library, environment) as a whole, and allows the engineer to evaluate the dependencies both during the original design as well as later when modifications are being considered.

5.2 Symbology

Each class is represented on the dependency diagram by a class box, with the published operations and logical components omitted. The name of the class appears in the bar at the top of the box. Each non-class friend module is represented by a simple rectangle labeled with the name of the module. This notation is illustrated in Figure 5.2.1.

Connectors are drawn between the classes and friend modules in the following manner:

> If any module within a class invokes a published operation of another class, draw a single-line connector (client-server connector) from the class containing the invoking module to the class whose operation is invoked.

> If any module within a class (call it Class A) either (1) invokes an internal operation of another class (Class B) or (2) makes direct access to the encapsulated data of Class B, draw a double-line connector (friend connector) from Class A to Class B.

> If a friend module invokes a published operation of a class, draw a client-server connector from the friend to the class.

> If a friend module invokes an internal operation of a class or makes direct access to the encapsulated data of a class, draw a friend connector from the friend to the class.

5.3 Alternative Representations and Automation

The dependency diagram lends itself to many alternative representations. The fundamental requirement is only that the client-server and friend connectors be distinguishable from one another, and that the classes and friend modules be represented by distinct symbols. For problems featuring a small number of classes, we find it useful to show the published operations on the dependency diagram and to depict the dependencies in more detail, showing exactly which published operations are invoked by other classes (Figure 9.3.8 of Chapter 9).

The dependency diagram summarizes certain invocations and data accesses that are represented on the class structure charts. Therefore, if the class structure charts are prepared first, the dependency diagram can be mechanically generated. Alternatively, if the dependency diagram and class structure charts are prepared in parallel, a consistency check is required.

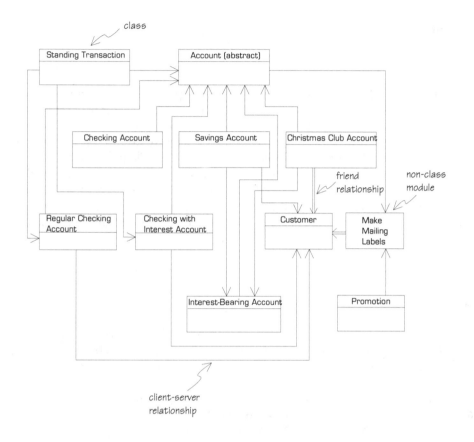

Figure 5.2.1: Dependency Diagram. Christmas Club Account is a friend class of the Customer class, while Making Mailing Labels is a friend module of Customer.

In an automated system, it would be desirable to provide a lower level, more detailed look at the dependencies between classes and friend modules. The dependency diagram as described here would provide an overview, while a "zoom view" of any particular class or friend module on the diagram would allow the user to see exactly which published operation, internal module or encapsulated data was being accessed by whom.

6. Inheritance Diagram

6.1 Purpose

The purpose of the inheritance diagram is to depict the inheritance relationships that pertain between the classes of a single program, library, or environment. The inheritance diagram is intended for use by a designer who wishes to construct or modify an inheritance structure or to modify the classes embedded in the structure. It is also of aid to a developer who uses the classes
in the structure, in that it allows him or her to understand the logical data structure that is accumulated up the hierarchy as a result of creating an instance at a low level. In addition, the inheritance diagram is helpful during debugging, since it presents the information required to analyze the effect of a polymorphic invocation.

6.2 Symbology

Each class is represented on the inheritance diagram by the class box of the class diagram. All of the detail internal to the class box is retained, but the external woks and parameter lines are omitted.

Only those classes that have inheritance relationships with other classes appear on the inheritance diagram. Any class that does not participate in an inheritance relationship with another class is omitted.

Inheritance relationships between classes are represented by the subtype-supertype notation of OOA. This notation is illustrated in Figure 6.2.1. Note that the notation allows for multiple inheritance.

6.3 Alternative Representation and Automation

Several alternative representations are reasonable for depicting the inheritance connections. If the subtype-supertype connector shown in Figure 6.2.1 is not available, we would suggest substituting a separate connector directed from the parent class to each child class.

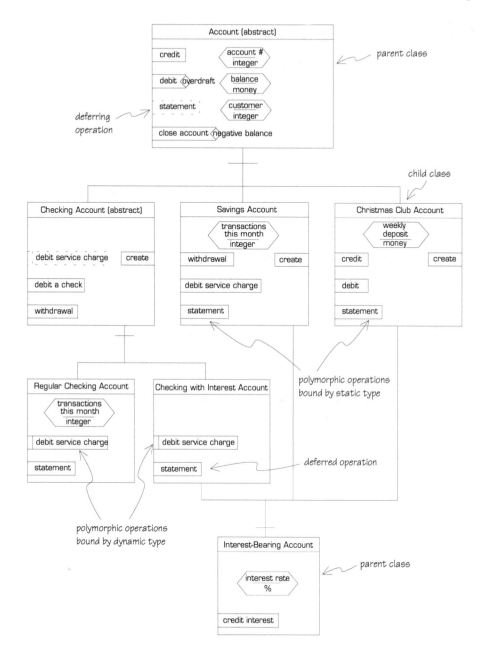

Figure 6.2.1: Inheritance Diagram. Account is the parent class of Checking Account, Savings Account, and Christmas Club Account.

References

[1] Grady Booch, *Object-Oriented Design with Applications*, Benjamin/Cummings Publishing Company, Redwood City, Calif. 1990.

[2] R. J. A. Buhr, *System Design with Ada*, Prentice Hall, Englewood Cliffs, N.J., 1984.

[3] Bertrand Meyer, *Object-Oriented Software Construction*, Prentice Hall International (UK) Ltd., Hemel Hempstead, 1988.

[4] Meilir Page-Jones, *A Practical Guide to Structured Systems Design*, Yourdon Press, New York, 1980.

[5] David K. Taylor and Alan Hecht, "Experiences Using CASE for Object-Oriented Design with C++," *Computer Language*, Miller-Freeman Publications, November 1990.

[6] Anthony J. Wasserman, Peter A. Pircher, and Robert J. Muller, "The Object-Oriented Structured Design Notation for Software Design Representation," *Computer*, Vol. 23, No. 3, IEEE Computer Society, March 1990.

[7] Fred Wild, *Ada Structure Graphs in Perspective: The Do's and Don'ts*, Cadre Technologies, Providence, R.I., 1988.

[8] Edward Yourdon and Larry L. Constantine, *Structured Design*, Yourdon Press, New York, 1975.

Using Object-Oriented Analysis with DOD-STD-2167A

This appendix provides guidelines for software developers to use in producing Software Requirements Analysis documentation compliant with DOD-STD-2167A on a project employing Object-Oriented Analysis. We assume here that the reader is generally familiar with the 2167A standard and its terminology.

1. Introduction

1.1 Why is This Report Necessary?

It is well understood that DOD-STD-2167A does not make any explicit statement on the kind of software development methodology to be employed on a project coming under its guidance. However, when this standard and its predecessor (DOD-STD-2167) were being developed, most systematic software development methods were fundamentally based on the concept of function. This historical orientation was reflected in 2167 directly in the wording of the Data Item Descriptions (DIDs), as well as indirectly in their structure.

This appendix is based on portions of a 1989 report entitled *"Documentation Guidelines for Ada Object-Oriented Development under 2167A"* prepared by Fredrick N. Hill, Stephen J. Mellor, Klancy de Nevers and Sally Shlaer of Project Technology, Inc. The material presented here has been updated to reflect the most recent definitions of the OOA work products.

The work was funded by the U.S. Army Project Manager FATDS, Fort Monmouth, New Jersey through Technical Evaluation Research, Inc., Little Silver, New Jersey.

The revision of the standard to DOD-STD-2167A was in part an attempt to open the door to other non-function-based methodologies. In this revision, certain wording was changed to move away from the function-based view: for example, the SRS DID is now organized around "capabilities" rather than "functions," which appeared in 2167. Nonetheless, traces of the original function-based orientation remain in the DIDs. While the essential organizing concept of the SRS is now called capability, capability still has an intrinsically functional nature with no fundamental connection to data. As a result, data elements are described as if they were isolated and free-floating atoms: repeatedly the DIDs ask for data to be correlated, element by element, with other conceptual entities.

However, in the object-oriented development paradigm, the essential organizing concept is the typical unspecified instance: the object of OOA or the class in C++. This concept links data and function in an integrated whole, and so provides an organization fundamentally different from that implicit in the DIDs.

This poses a significant problem for projects employing an object-oriented development strategy, in that it is not obvious how to organize object-oriented development documentation in a manner consistent with both the language and the intent of 2167A. This report provides a solution to this problem based on the work products of OOA.

1.2 Assumptions

An object-oriented approach to software development can be introduced into a project at various points in the development process. For our purposes here, we have assumed a typical situation in which the object-oriented development approach is selected to begin with the Software Requirements Analysis activity. It is therefore assumed that the SSS and SSDD have already been prepared. No other assumptions are made with respect to the SSS and SSDD.

1.3 Contents

The following sections examine the DIDs for the SRS and the IRS and lay out guidelines for repackaging (and sometimes supplementing) the work products of OOA so as to produce documentation in conformance with the DIDs.

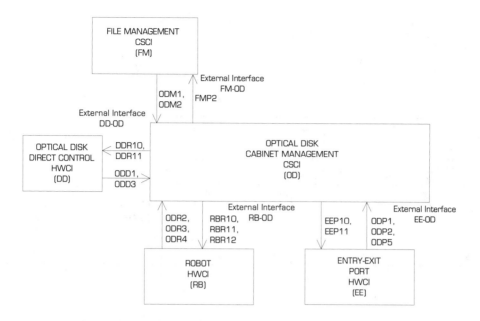

Figure 2.2.1: The external interfaces in which this CSCI participates are identified on a Subsystem Communication Model.

The remainder of this report is organized by paragraph number of the SRS and IRS. *Only those paragraphs specifically affected by the object-oriented approach are listed.* For ease of reference, the directive material from the referenced DID is quoted and enclosed in boxes. Where we recommend tailoring the language of the DID, that tailoring is indicated by strikethrough (~~strikethrough~~).

The following sections are provided, where pertinent, for each SRS and IRS paragraph treated:

- What to Supply. Explains what work products to supply for the referenced paragraph.

- What to Tailor Out. Discusses the reasoning behind the recommended tailoring.

- Meeting the Requirements of the DID. Discusses how the supplied work products meet (or do not meet) the requirements of the DID.

DATA ACCESSES FOR EXTERNAL INTERFACE FM-OD			
Data (Object.Attribute)	Data Source CSCI/HWCI	Data Destination CSCI/HWCI	Data Destination (Reader object)

EVENT LIST FOR EXTERNAL INTERFACE FM-OD						
Event Label	Event Meaning	Data	Event Source CSCI/HWCI	Event Source State Model	Event Destination CSCI/HWCI	Event Destination State Model

Figure 2.2.2: An external interface is defined in terms of the data accesses and events that cross the interface.

2. The Software Requirements Specification (SRS)

2.1 SRS Paragraph 1.3: Document Overview

> 10.1.3.3 Document overview. This paragraph shall be numbered 1.3 and shall summarize the purpose and contents of this document.

What to Supply

1. If the CSCI corresponds to a small domain in OOA, include the **mission statement** of the domain. If it corresponds to a subsystem, include the **subsystem description**.

2.2 SRS Paragraph 3.1: CSCI External Interface

10.1.5.1 CSCI external interface requirements. This paragraph shall be numbered 3.1 and shall identify the external interfaces of the CSCI. An external interface diagram similar to Figure 1 may be used to aid in this description. Each external interface shall be identified by ~~name and~~ project-unique identifier and a brief description of each interface shall be provided. Any identifying documentation, such as an Interface Control Document or Interface Requirements Specification, shall be referenced for each interface.

What to Supply

1. **Subsystem Communication Model.** Supply a Subsystem Communication Model in which each CSCI, HWCI, or critical item is represented as a subsystem. Provide a project-unique identifier for each external interface by concatenating the subsystem prefix letters assigned to the CIs on either side of the interface, as shown in Figure 2.2.1.

2. **Interface Description.** As subparagraph 3.1.k, describe the kth external interface by listing all events and data accesses that cross the interface. This can be done by extraction from the Event List and State Process Table to produce tables such as those shown in Figure 2.2.2.

What to Tailor Out

Providing a name (in addition to the project-unique identifier) for each external interface adds no value to the analysis. Accordingly, we suggest that this requirement be deleted.

2.3 SRS Paragraph 3.2: CSCI Capability Requirements

10.1.5.2 CSCI capability requirements. This paragraph shall be numbered 3.2·and shall identify, in the subparagraphs that follow, all of the capability requirements that the CSCI must satisfy. If the system of which the CSCI is a part can exist in various system states and modes as documented in the system specification, this paragraph shall identify each such state and mode and shall correlate each CSCI capability to those states and modes. A table may be used to depict this correlation.

A CSCI capability is to be identified with a state model in OOA.

CORRELATION OF SYSTEM STATES AND OBJECT STATES			
System State	System Mode	State Model	State Number

Figure 2.3.1: Table presenting the correlation of states of the OOA state models with the states and modes of the system as specified in the SSS.

What to Supply

1. **State Correlation.** The states and modes given in the system specification are to be correlated with the states of the OOA state models. This may or may not be an easy correlation, depending on the original basis used to establish the states and modes. The example given in the SSS DID suggests that the system states and modes may correspond fairly directly to states of objects appearing near the top of the Object Communication Model for (probably one) CSCI.

    To record the correlation, consider how each system state and mode is established. Trace through the thread of control that begins with establishing that system state and mode. Record in a table (as in Figure 2.3.1) all states of all state models encountered until activity terminates on all legs of the thread of control.

2.4 SRS Subparagraph 3.2.x: (Capability name and project-unique identifier).

10.1.5.2.1 (Capability name and project-unique identifier). This subparagraph shall be numbered 3.2.x (beginning with 3.2.1), shall identify the CSCI capability by name and project-unique identifier and shall state the purpose of the capability ~~and its performance in measurable terms~~. This subparagraph shall identify and state the purpose of each input and output associated with the capability. ~~This subparagraph shall identify the allocated or derived requirements that the capability satisfies or partially satisfies.~~ If the capability can be more clearly specified by decomposing it into constituent capabilities, the requirements for each constituent capability shall be provided as one or more subparagraphs. Each constituent capability shall be assigned a project-unique identifier that is derived from the identifier of the parent capability.

The project-unique identifier for the capability (state model) is the state model key letter that was assigned in OOA. The name of the capability is the name of the state model.

A constituent capability is to be identified with a single state of the state model. The project-unique identifier of a constituent capability is <state model key letter>.<state number>.

What to Supply

1. **Statement of Purpose.** For a state model other than an Assigner state model, the purpose can be stated as "To formalize the dynamic behavior of <object name>". A reference should also be made to the object description in subparagraph 3.4.1.<object number> of the SRS.

    If the state model is an Assigner state model, its purpose will be to regulate communication between two objects. The purpose can be stated in terms of regulating such communication for the purposes of allocation of resources, holding requests until they can be serviced, or the like.

2. The **State Transition Diagram** for the state model. The STD must show all event labels, meanings, and the data carried by each event.

3. A **State Transition Table** representation of the same state model.

4. **Actions.** If there is insufficient space on the State Transition Diagram to depict the actions adequately, express the actions in pseudocode within subparagraph 3.2.x as follows:

    Action for State 1: [supply pseudocode]

    Action for State 2: [supply pseudocode]

    . . .

5. **Action Data Flow Diagrams.** (As sub-subparagraphs, numbered 3.2.x.<state number>): Supply the action data flow diagrams (ADFDs) for each state of state model x.

Meeting the Requirements of the DID

"...state the purpose of the capability". Given in the Statement of Purpose.

INTERNAL INTERFACE IDENTIFICATION TABLE											
State Model Name	State Model Number	1	2	3	4	5	6	7	8	9	10
	1		2				State Model Numbers				
	2	none		3							
	3	1	none		4						
	4	none	none	2		5					
	5	none	3	4	5		6				
	6	none	none	6	7	8		7			
	7	none	none	none	none	9	10		8		
	8	none	11	none	none	none	none	12		9	
	9	13	none	none	14	15	none	none	16		10
	10	none	none	none	none	none	17	18	none	none	

Figure 2.5.1: The Internal Interface Identification Table provides a reference number for each interface between the state models of this CSCI.

"state . . . performance in measurable terms." In the object-oriented paradigm, each object responds to different events at different times, taking varying amounts of time to make the required response. Only a portion of the capability is typically involved in producing each response. The performance of the capability taken as a whole is therefore not well-defined in the object-oriented world.

In addition, because many objects can be involved in making something happen in the system, performance of a single action of a single object is not very meaningful viewed in isolation. We therefore suggest that this phrase of the DID be removed by tailoring. More meaningful measures and estimates of performance will be covered in SRS Paragraph 3.6, Timing and Sizing Requirements.

"identify . . . each input and output associated with the capability." There are two kinds of inputs and outputs associated with a capability: The events (including the data carried with each event), and the accesses made to data of other objects. The events and their associated data appear on the state transition diagram. The accesses appear in the action descriptions (either on the STD or in item 4 above).

"state the purpose of each input and output associated with the capability." The event meanings state the purpose of each input and output event. The names of the accessor processes (as shown on the ADFDs) state the purpose of the accessed data as seen by this capability.

". . . identify the allocated or derived requirements . . ." This sentence should be deleted by tailoring, since its intent will be satisfied by SRS paragraph 3.12, Requirements Traceability.

". . . the requirements for each constituent capability shall be provided . . ." These are provided in the data flow diagrams of sub-paragraph 3.2.x.<state number>.

2.5 SRS Paragraph 3.3: CSCI Internal Interfaces

> 10.1.5.3 CSCI Internal Interfaces. This paragraph shall be numbered 3.3 and shall identify the interfaces between the capabilities identified above. Each internal interface shall be identified by ~~name and~~ project-unique identifier and ~~a brief description of each interface shall be provided, including~~ a summary of the information transmitted over the interface. Internal interface diagrams depicting data flow, control flow, and other relevant information may be used to aid in this description.

What to Supply

1. **Internal Interface Identification Table.** The purpose of this table is to declare systematically which state models have interfaces between them and to provide a local reference number for each such defined interface. The table has the form shown in Figure 2.5.1.

   The italicized entries provide either a local internal interface number (that will be used in the next item) or the statement "none," meaning that there is no direct interface between the two particular state models.

2. **Object Communication Model.** Provide the object communication model to depict the asynchronous communication between the capabilities.

3. **Object Access Model.** Provide the object access model to depict the synchronous communication between the capabilities.

4. **Information Transmitted over the Interface** (as subparagraph 3.3.k). For each interface defined in the Internal Interface Identification Table, provide a project-unique identifier for the internal interface in the form < subsystem prefix for this CSCI > - k, where k is the local internal interface number from the Internal Interface Identification Table.

   Describe the asynchronous aspect of the internal interface by listing all events (event label, event meaning, event data items, event source, and event destination) that have one of the two state models as "Event Source"

EVENTS OF INTERNAL INTERFACE OD - <local internal interface number>				
Event Label	Event Meaning	Data	Event Source	Event Destination

Figure 2.5.2: Table depicting the events that cross an internal interface of this CSCI.

and the other state model as "Event Destination" in the OOA Event List. This information can all be mechanically extracted from the event list and expressed in a table such as that shown in Figure 2.5.2.

Then describe the synchronous aspect of the internal interface by listing all accessors assigned to one object and invoked by an action of the other object's state model. This information can be extracted from the state process table and ADFDs and presented in a table as in Figure 2.5.3. Fill out the columns as follows

    (1) Name of the object to which the accessor process is assigned (derived from column 1 of the State Process Table).

    (2) Name of the state model which invokes the process (from column 4 of the State Process Table).

    (3) Process name (column 3 of the State Process Table).

    (4) Attributes input to the process via data flows other than from a data store (from any ADFD that invokes the process).

    (5) Attributes output by the process via data flows other than from a data store (from any ADFD that invokes the process).

Meeting the Requirements of the DID

"identify the interfaces between the capabilities." Provided by the Internal Interface Identification Table.

"Each internal interface shall be identified by name and project-unique identifier." The project-unique identifier is provided by Item 4 above. There is no point in naming the internal interfaces; we therefore recommend that this requirement be deleted.

"a brief description of each interface shall be provided." In the OOA paradigm, the concept of a description of the interface is not meaningful except in terms of the information transmitted. The requirement for a description should therefore be tailored out.

". . . a summary of the information transmitted over the interface." The information given in the tables of item 4 above provides a complete statement (not a summary) of the information transmitted over the interface.

2.6 SRS Paragraph 3.4: CSCI Data Element Requirements

10.1.5.4 CSCI data element requirements. This paragraph shall be numbered 3.4 and shall specify the information identified below, as applicable.
a. For data elements internal to the CSCI:
    (1) Assign a project-unique identifier to the data element
    (2) Provide a brief description of the data element
    (3) Identify the Units of measure required for the data element, such as sec onds, meters, kilohertz, etc.
    (4) Identify the limit/range of values required for the data element (for constants provide the actual value)
    (5) Identify the accuracy required for the data element
    (6) Identify the precision or resolution required for the data element in terms of significant digits
    ~~(7) For data elements of the CSCI's internal interfaces:~~
        ~~- Identify the interface by name and project-unique identifier~~
        ~~- Identify the source capability of the data element by name and project-unique identifier~~
        ~~- Identify the destination capability of the data element by name and project-unique identifier.~~
~~b. For data elements of the CSCI's external interfaces:~~
    ~~(1) Identify the data elements by project-unique identifier~~
    ~~(2) Identify the interface by name and project-unique identifier~~
    ~~(3) Identify the source or destination capability, as applicable, by name and project-unique identifier~~
    ~~(4) Reference the Interface Requirements Specification in which the interface is specified.~~

A data element corresponds to an attribute in OOA.

What to Supply

1. Supply the **Information Structure Diagram**.

ACCESSES ACROSS INTERNAL INTERFACE - <local internal interface number>				
accessor assigned to [1]	accessor invoked from [2]	accessor (process) name [3]	inputs [4]	outputs [5]

Figure 2.5.3: Table depicting the synchronous data accesses that take place across an internal interface of this CSCI.

2. The remainder of the information model is best handled by being structured into subparagraphs and sub-subparagraphs as described below. Note that this produces an organization equivalent to the **OOA Objects and Attributes Document** and the **Relationships Document**.

   3.4.1.k (Object name). Provide the object description for object number k within this CSCI, a list of all attributes of the object in order of attribute number, and a list of all candidate identifiers for the object.

   3.4.1.k.j (Attribute name). Provide the attribute description and domain description for the jth attribute of object k. Provide also a statement of the accuracy and precision required for the attribute.

   3.4.2.k (Relationship name of relationship number k). The relationship description, form of the relationship (multiplicity and conditionality), and statement of how the relationship is formalized in referential attributes or by composition.

What to Tailor Out

Delete item a(7), since this information has already been provided in SRS subparagraphs 3.3.k (in two tables in each such subparagraph).

Delete item b, since this information has already been provided in two tables in SRS paragraph 3.1.

Meeting the Requirements of the DID

The remaining requirement items of this paragraph are met as follows:

   a(1) The full name of the attribute (Object_name.attribute_name) provides a project-unique identifier for the data element.

INSTALLATION-DEPENDENT ATTRIBUTES		
Object Name	Attribute Name	Capability

Figure 2.7.1: Table depicting the installation-dependent attributes of this CSCI.

a(2) Satisfied by the attribute descriptions of subparagraph 3.4.1.k.j

a(3) Satisfied by the domain descriptions of subparagraph 3.4.1.k.j

a(4) Covered by the domain descriptions of subparagraph 3.4.1.k.j

a(5) Also covered in subparagraph 3.4.1.k.j

a(6) Also covered in subparagraph 3.4.1.k.j

2.7 SRS Subparagraph 3.5.1: Installation-Dependent Data

10.1.5.5.1 Installation-dependent data. This subparagraph shall be numbered 3.5.1 and shall describe the site-unique data required by each installation. Examples of such data are: site latitude and longitude, radar ranges and areas of coverage, and prescribed safety limits. In addition, this subparagraph shall identify the CSCI capabilities in which these data are used.

What to Supply

1. Identify any such installation-dependent attributes and enter them in a table as shown in Figure 2.7.1. Fill out the rest of the table by examining:

   (a) The Event List. Find all events that carry this attribute. The capability using the attribute is given as the Event Destination.

   (b) The State Process Table. Find all read accesses that refer to this attribute. The capability using the attribute is given in the column labeled "State Model."

   (c) If the installation-dependent attribute is an attribute of an object that has a state model, list the state model name as the capability.

The table should then be sorted in order of object name, then attribute name, and finally capability name.

2.8 SRS Subparagraph 3.5.2: Operational Parameters

> 10.1.5.5.2 Operational parameters. This subparagraph shall be numbered 3.5.2 and shall describe parameters required by the CSCI that may vary within a specified range according to operational needs. Examples of such data are: allowable trajectory deviations, navigation set model numbers, airplane performance characteristics, interact/isolation of sorties, missile performance characteristics. This subparagraph shall identify the CSCI capabilities in which these data are used.

What to Supply

A table exactly like that described for subparagraph 3.5.1, but containing instead those attributes that meet the definition of operational parameters.

2.9 SRS Paragraph 3.6: Sizing and Timing Requirements

> 10.1.5.6 Sizing and timing requirements. This paragraph shall be numbered 3.6 and shall specify the amount and, if applicable, location of internal and auxiliary memory and the amount of processing time allocated to the CSCI. This paragraph shall specify the resources required of both memory and the central processing unit (CPU) for the CSCI.

What to Tailor Out

This paragraph is problematic in that it asks for information that is largely dependent on the design scheme chosen. This seems inappropriate when the SRS is viewed as an analysis document, since the requested information is not known at analysis time.

In addition, the paragraph does not ask for certain information that is obtainable and crucial for the success of the system. The language of the DID is more focussed on regulating the construction of the software to make sure it fits inside the computer(s) chosen, rather than on determining what requirements the system users will place on the system (event rates, response times, throughput requirements). We believe this is a weakness: One cannot evaluate the quality of a design (to be revealed in the SDD) unless one has performance requirements stated separately from that design.

ATTRIBUTE SIZES		
Object Name	Attribute Name	Bytes per Instance
Slot	Slot ID	2
Slot	Status	1
. . .	. . .	. . .
Disk	Disk ID	10
. . .	. . .	. . .

OBJECT SIZES		
Object Name	Number of Instance	Bytes Total
Slot	50	750
Disk	14,000	560,000
Robot	1	54

EVENT RATES AND RESPONSE TIMES			
Unsolicited Event		Response(s)	Response Times
Label	Rate		
E100	20/hour	Mounted from external library	5 minutes after cabinet space available
		Mounted when unowned in cabinet	10 seconds
		Mounted when owned in cabinet	10 seconds after becoming unowned
E101	20/hour	none required	not applicable

Figure 2.9.1: Tables depicting sizing and timing requirements derived from the analysis.

Another observation: In the last sentence of the DID paragraph, there appears to be an assumption that a CSCI will be implemented on one CPU. This may not be a good assumption when the CSCI is based on an object-oriented partitioning.

We recommend that the specific provisions of the paragraph be tailored out, but that the paragraph itself be left in place.

What to Supply

Interpreting the paragraph as a requirement to provide timing and sizing information pertinent to making design decisions, we suggest that the following be supplied (see Figure 2.9.1):

1. **Object and Attribute Sizes.** Provide tables depicting the number of instances of each object and the amount of space required to store the logical data structure representing each instance. Note that this is only an estimate of the actual amount of physical storage space required, since this depends on the physical data structures that are determined as part of a design.

237

2. **Event Rates and Response Times.** State the average rate at which unsolicited events are expected from outside the CSCI. Service of the events at the expected rate is a true requirement on the CSCI, and so should appear in the SRS.

For each unsolicited event, there may be an acceptable response time. If such is known, that information should be recorded and passed to the designer.

2.10 SRS Paragraph 3.12: Requirements Traceability

> 10.1.5.12 Requirements traceability. This paragraph shall be numbered 3.12 and shall contain a mapping of the engineering requirements in this specification to the requirements applicable to this CSCI in the SSS, PIDS, or CIDS. This paragraph shall also provide a mapping of the allocation of the CSCI requirements from the SSS, PIDS, or CIDS to the engineering requirements in this specification.

The engineering requirements in the SRS are expressed in terms of the elements of the OOA formalism: objects, events, and state models. We assume that the requirements from the SSS, PIDS, or CIDS have been assigned some kind of identifiers for the purposes of requirements traceability. Then, to satisfy this paragraph of the DID, fill out the table of Figure 2.10.1.

The table should be presented in two sortings:

(1) sorted by SSS requirement number (column 1); and

(2) sorted by column 2 followed by column 3.

3. The Interface Requirements Specification (IRS)

3.1 IRS Paragraph 3.1: Interface Diagrams

> 10.1.5.1 Interface diagrams. This paragraph shall be numbered 3.1 and shall identify the interfaces among the CSCIs, HWCIs and critical items to which this specification applies. One or more interface diagrams, as appropriate, shall be provided to depict the interfaces. Each interface shall be identified by ~~name and~~ project-unique identifier.

Each CSCI, HWCI and critical item shall be given a short project-unique alphabetic identifier. Each interface shall be given a project-unique identifier

SSS Requirement Number [1]	OOA Entity Type [2]	OOA Entity Name [3]

[1] Fill in the requirement number from the SSS, PIDS, or CIDS

[2] Fill in "object", "relationship", "event", or "state model"

[3] Fill in the object name, relationship number, event label, or state model name, as appropriate.

Figure 2.10.1: Table depicting the correlation between requirements stated in the SSS, PIDS, or CIDS and the OOA elements of this CSCI.

constructed from the identifiers of the CIs on either side of the interface: <CSCI identifier> - <HWCI identifier>.

What to Supply

1. **Subsystem Communication Model.** Supply a Subsystem Communication Model of the same type as was supplied for SRS paragraph 3.1, but include all CSCIs, HWCIs, and critical items to which this specification applies.

2. **Subsystem Access Model.** Provide a corresponding Subsystem Access Model covering the same CSCIs, HWCIs, and critical items.

What to Tailor Out

Providing a name for each external interface (in addition to the project unique identifier) adds no value to the analysis; accordingly we suggest that this requirement be deleted.

3.2 IRS Paragraph 3.x: (Interface name and project-unique identifier)

10.1.5.2 (Interface ~~name and~~ project-unique identifier). This paragraph shall be numbered 3.x (beginning with 3.2) and shall identify an interface by ~~name and~~ project-unique identifier, ~~and shall state its purpose~~. This paragraph shall be divided into the following subparagraphs to specify the requirements for the interface and for the data transmitted across the interface.

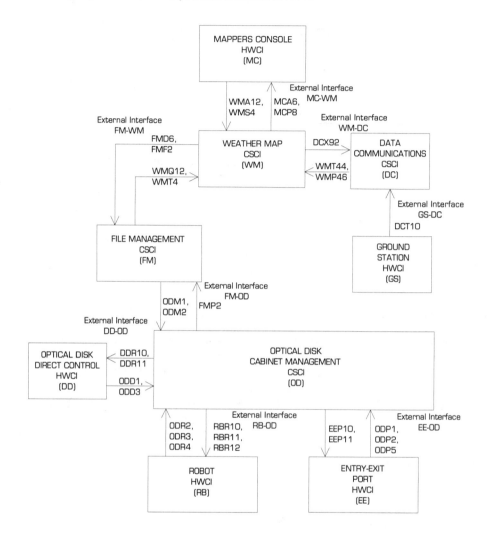

Figure 3.1.1: Subsystem Communication Model used to satisfy
requirements of IRS paragraph 3.1.

The project-unique identifiers required are the same as those shown on the figure of IRS paragraph 3.1.

What to Tailor Out

Remove the references to interface name for consistency with IRS paragraph 3.1.

In the object-oriented paradigm, the purpose of an interface is only to transmit the events and their associated data. We suggest that the requirement for a separate statement of purpose be deleted, since the intent of the requirement is fulfilled by subsequent subparagraphs of the IRS.

3.3 IRS Paragraph 3.x.1: Interface Requirements

> 10.1.5.2.1 Interface requirements. This subparagraph shall be numbered 3.x.1 (beginning with 3.2.1) and shall specify the following, as applicable:
> a. Whether the interfacing CSCIs are to execute concurrently or sequentially. If concurrently, the method of inter-CSCI synchronization to be used.
> b. The communication protocol to be used for the interface.
> c. The priority level of the interface.

What to Supply

1. **Analysis of Concurrency.** The general assumption of Object-Oriented Analysis is that all objects (and therefore all CSCIs, HWCIs and critical items) execute concurrently except when explicitly serialized by means of events. The method of synchronization is by the events.

   We recommend that a short description be provided for each interface that discusses which event is transmitted across the interface first, which of the interface events might be generated back in response, and any subsequent interaction by means of events. This amounts to an informal description of the application protocol for the interface. For a formal description of the application protocol, refer to the associated state models (paragraphs 3.2.k of the SRSs for the participating CSCIs).

2. **Statement of Communications Protocol.** The communications protocol, if known, should be specified. Note that in an object-oriented system, there

can be external interfaces that lie entirely within a CPU. In this case, the communications protocol will be simply the internal event-transmission mechanism specified in the design.

Meeting the Requirements of the DID

Whether the interfacing CSCIs are to execute concurrently or sequentially. If concurrently, the method of inter-CSCI synchronization to be used. Satisfied by the Analysis of Concurrency.

The communication protocol to be used for the interface. Given in the Statement of Communications Protocol.

The priority level of the interface. There is no concept of priority of interface (or priority of event) in object-oriented analysis and design. If the concept can be made well-defined for a particular project, respond appropriately; otherwise we recommend tailoring out this requirement.

3.4 IRS Paragraph 3.x.2: Data Requirements

10.1.5.2.2 Data requirements. This paragraph shall be numbered 3.x.2 (beginning with 3.2.2) and shall specify, in a data element definition table similar to Table 1, the following information, as applicable, for each data element transmitted across the interface:
  a. A project-unique identifier for the data element
  b. A brief description of the data element
  c. The CSCI, HWCI, or critical item that is the source of the data element
  d. The CSCI(s), HWCI(s), or critical item(s) that are the users of the data element
  e. The Units of measure required for the data element, such as seconds, meters, kilohertz, etc.
  f. The limit/range of values required for the data element (for constants provide the actual value)
  g. The accuracy required for the data element
  h. The precision or resolution required for the data element in terms of significant digits.

What to Supply

1. Supply the table shown in Figure 3.4.1. For column [3], supply a short description of the domain of the attribute. For column [4], provide the CSCI name to which the <object name> object is assigned, and the SRS subparagraph number that defines the attribute. Columns [5] and [6] are

INTERFACE DATA ELEMENT DEFINITION TABLE for interface <interface identifier>								
Object Name [1]	Attribute Name [2]	Description [3]	Reference [4]	Source CSCI [5]	Destination CSCI [6]	Unit of Measure [7]	Accuracy [8]	Precision/ Resolution [9]

Figure 3.4.1: Table depicting the data elements transmitted across an external interface.

used to record all transmissions of <object name>.<attribute name> across the interface. Columns [5] and [6] enter the source and destination of the data element. Note that there can be multiple entries in columns [5] and [6] for a single entry of <object name>.<attribute name>. Columns [7], [8] and [9] can be filled in from the SRS subparagraph referenced in column [4].

Meeting the Requirements of the DID

The items required by this paragraph are supplied as follows:

    a. Supplied by columns [1] and [2].
    b. Column [3]
    c. Column [6]
    d. Column [7]
    e. Column [8]
    f. Column [9]
    g. Column [10]

References

[1] *Defense System Software Development*, Document DOD-STD-2167A, U. S. Department of Defense, 1988.

[2] *A Tailoring Guide for DOD-STD-2167A, Defense System Software Development*, Document DOD-HDBK-287, U. S. Department of Defense, 1988 (Draft).

Index

A

Abnormal behavior. *See* Failure
  analysis
Abstract class   179, 217
Accessor   125-126, 128, 174, 176,
  184, 187
Action   5, 9, 36, 44–49, 57
  design for   186–188, 189
  events, and   47
  rule   105–106
  thread of control, in   95
  time, and   47, 105–106. *See*
    also Action time
Action data flow diagram   9, 112–
  122, 132
Action time   98–99
Active class   175–177
  class structure chart   183–188
Actor   89
Ada   163, 219
ADFD. *See* Action data flow
  diagram

Agent   93
Application class   171–179
  class structure chart   181–189
Application domain   135
Architectural domain   136–
  137, 161
Assigner   73
  and ADFDs   127
  key letter   73
  passive classes, and   192
Assigner class   177–179
  class structure chart   189
Associative object   25–31, 68–
  69, 72–76
Asynchronous communica-
  tion   131
Attribute   3
  accumulation of   61
  current state. *See* Current state:
    attribute
  definition of   14
  descriptions   18–19, 31
  determinant   101–102
  domain   14–15
  description   18–19

245

S

Service domain   135
  inheritance, and   180–181
Shared data area   223
Simulation   101–104
Simultaneous interpretation of
    concurrency   104
Smalltalk   215, 218, 219
Solicited event   93
Specification
  event   44
Specification object   13, 62
Splicing   59
State   5, 35, 38–41
  creation   39
  current   41–42, 46
  final   41
  initial, for simulation   101
  name   39
  number   39
State machine
  initialization   177, 179, 183,
    189
  mechanism   164–169
  vs. state model   38
State model   3–4, 9, 33
  lifecycles, as   34–38
  vs. state machine   38
State process table   129–130, 132
State transition diagram   34–38
  lifecycles, for   34–38
State transition table   50–52
Static binding   219–220
Subsystem   2, 9, 145
  access model   154
  communication model   151–152
  definition of   146–148
  descriptions   151
  notebook   158–159

relationship model   151
Subsystem communication
    model   5, 9
Subtype migration   57–58
Subtype-supertype   28, 179
  lifecycles   57–60
Synchronous communication   131
System state
  establishment of, for simula-
    tion   101

T

Tangible object   13
Terminator. *See* External entity
Test process   127, 129–131, 188
Thread of control   94–100, 136
Thread of control chart   97
Time   98–99, 104–107
  action   98–99
  action and   47
  dwell   98–99
  event and   47
  rules about   105–107, 192
Timer   52–54, 85, 170–171
  data store   113
  design for   191–192
  process   118
Transformation
  process   126–127, 128–129, 188
Transition   36, 50–52, 192
  class   164–165

U

Unconditional relationship   22–23
Unsolicited event   93
Unsolicited external event
  in simulation   101
Utility function   215

V

Virtual device   89
Virtual function   220

W

White box   55
Wok   217, 218, 221
  basis and ordering of   219
  conditional   220
Work product   9, 31, 64, 132
  action data flow diagram   9, 132
  design   192–193
  domain chart   9
  event list   65
  information model   9
  object access model   9, 132
  object communication model   9
  process description   9, 132
  project matrix   9, 154
  state model   9, 64
  state process table   132
  subsystem communication
    model   9
Write accessor   126

Project Technology Courses

Project Technology Inc., founded in 1984 by the authors, offers top quality courses and consulting in Object-Oriented Analysis and Recursive Design. These courses are intended for the practicing analyst and designer. Each course features extensive exercises that build up to a complete case study. Overview courses are also available.

Information Models

The focus of this course is on identifying and defining the semantic content of problem domains. Students learn how to extract expert knowledge from diverse engineering and technical disciplines and transform that knowledge into objects, attributes and relationships.

The course follows *Object-Oriented Systems Analysis: Modeling the World in Data.*

State and Process Models

The course shows how to formalize the dynamic behavior and interactions of objects using state models and action data flow diagrams. Topics include object lifecycles, dynamic relationships, contention problems, thread of control analysis, failure analysis and variation of requirements.

The course follows *Object Lifecycles: Modeling the World in States.*

Recursive Design

Recursive Design is an OOA-based system-level design method that incorporates a range of design architectures. The course covers object-oriented designs, functionally composed designs, real-time architectures and design mappings. Detailed transformations of analyses into design are featured.

The course is available in language-specific versions.

For more information about these and related courses, detach and mail this reply card, or call Project Technology at (510) 845-1484.

I am interested in receiving more information about:

☐ **Information Models**   ☐ **State and Process Models**

☐ **Recursive Design**   ☐ **Overview Courses**

NAME

COMPANY

DEPARTMENT/MAIL STOP

ADDRESS

CITY   STATE/PROVINCE   ZIP/POSTAL CODE

COUNTRY   PHONE

PROJECT TECHNOLOGY, INC.

2560 NINTH STREET

SUITE 214

BERKELEY, CA 94710